Color Me Whole

A MomPositive Coloring Book

Copyright © 2015 by Tammi Hoerner

The content of this book is for general instruction only.
Each person's physical, emotional, and spiritual condition is unique.
The instruction in this book is not intended to replace or interrupt the reader's relationship

with a physician or other professional.

Please consult your doctor for matters pertaining to your specific health and diet.

Written and Designed by Tammi Hoerner, INHC

ISBN: 978-1519360830

To contact the publisher, visit
www.headpositivemom.com

To contact the author, visit
www.headpositivemom.com

Welcome to the world of MomPositive, a place where living in a healthy body and living a creative life come together. I am so happy that you've joined me here.

In this MomPositive Coloring Book, I've brought together a daily journal complimented with a variety of images, words, and ideas that I hope invite you to relax, slow down, take a breath, and to get present. Studies show coloring can be as healthful as meditation, that it is an effective method of stress relief, and can be a way for you to center and ground yourself. Keeping a journal is supportive of reaching health goals, as well as tracking progress and working through your ideas and thoughts. Combined, I hope they bring you insight and space for growth and self discovery.

Through this book, as you work to find peace in your mind and heart, you are also inviting playfulness and nurturing creativity which so often in adult life is a neglected area of our being.

I hope you enjoy your time spent here and I hope it brings you peace, a smile, satisfaction, and that it inspires you to add more color to your every day.

My favorite tools to use when I color are colored pencils. As you begin to get comfortable here, you might find your own favorite tools—pencils, pens, crayons, even marker. If you choose to use marker, I suggest placing a piece of paper between your pages to prevent bleeding through to the next page.

A few thoughts to remember as you make your way through these journal pages and images...

- Enjoy yourself

- This can be fun, light, or meditative all ways are beneficial

- Try putting on relaxing music while you color to help you to relax more deeply

- Invite someone to color with you

- There aren't any rules, set your own as you go, or enjoy not having any!

- There isn't any right or wrong way to color, experiment with different colors and techniques—but most of all, enjoy yourself!

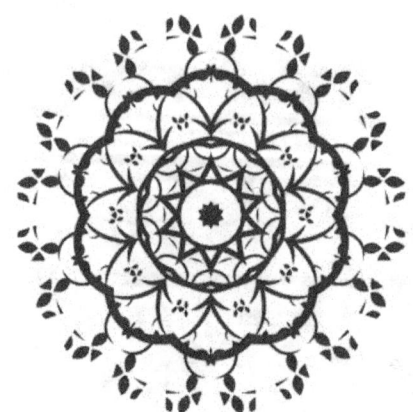

Wishing you colorful and happy days,

Tammi

Hopes and Dreams

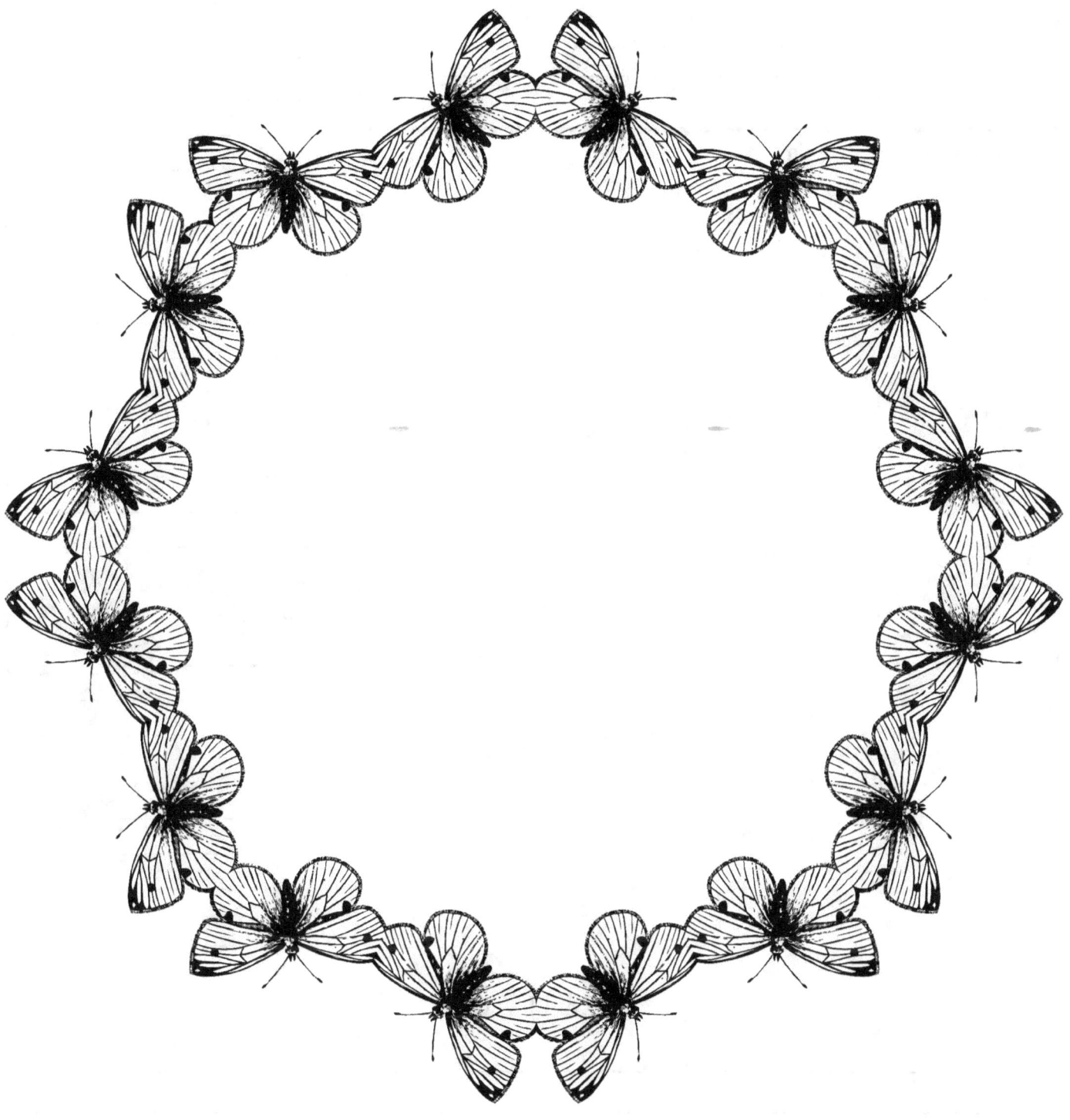

What are some of your greatest hopes and dreams for this life? For this world? For your loved ones? Take time to write them in the butterfly circle above.

Morning thoughts:

_____
_____
_____
_____
_____
_____
_____

DATE:
_____

Food

Water: IIII IIII IIII

Breakfast:

_____
_____
_____
_____

Lunch:

_____
_____
_____
_____

Dinner:

_____
_____
_____
_____

Snacks:

_____
_____

Notes:

_____
_____
_____

Goals & Intentions for today

1
2
3
4
5
6

GRATITUDE

REFLECTION

_____
_____
_____
_____
_____

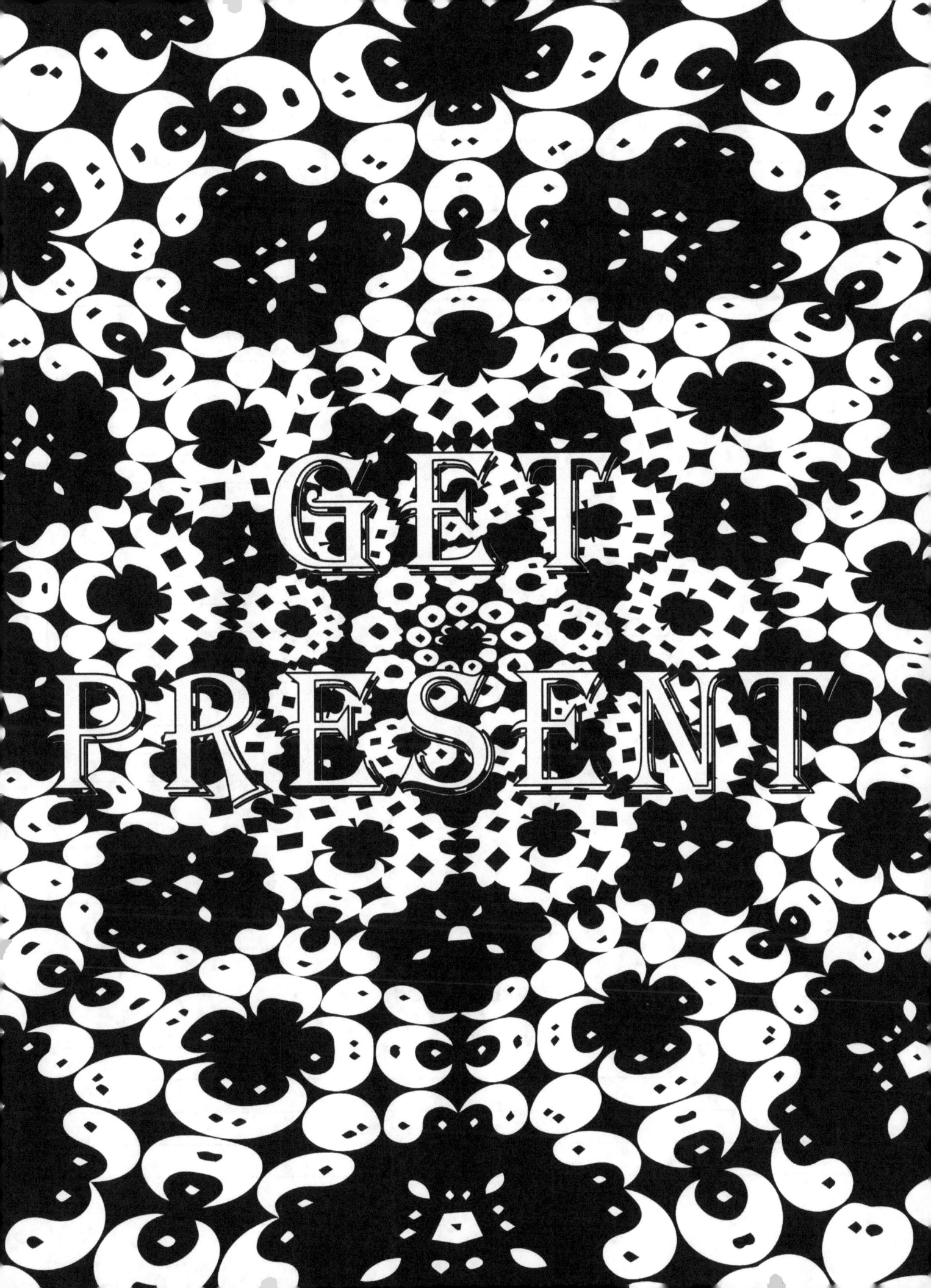

Morning thoughts:

_____
_____
_____
_____
_____
_____
_____

DATE:

_____

Goals & Intentions for today

1

2

3

4

5

6

GRATITUDE

Food

Water: IIII IIII IIII

Breakfast:

_____
_____
_____
_____

Lunch:

_____
_____
_____
_____

Dinner:

_____
_____
_____
_____

Snacks:

_____
_____

Notes:

_____
_____
_____

REFLECTION

_____
_____
_____
_____
_____

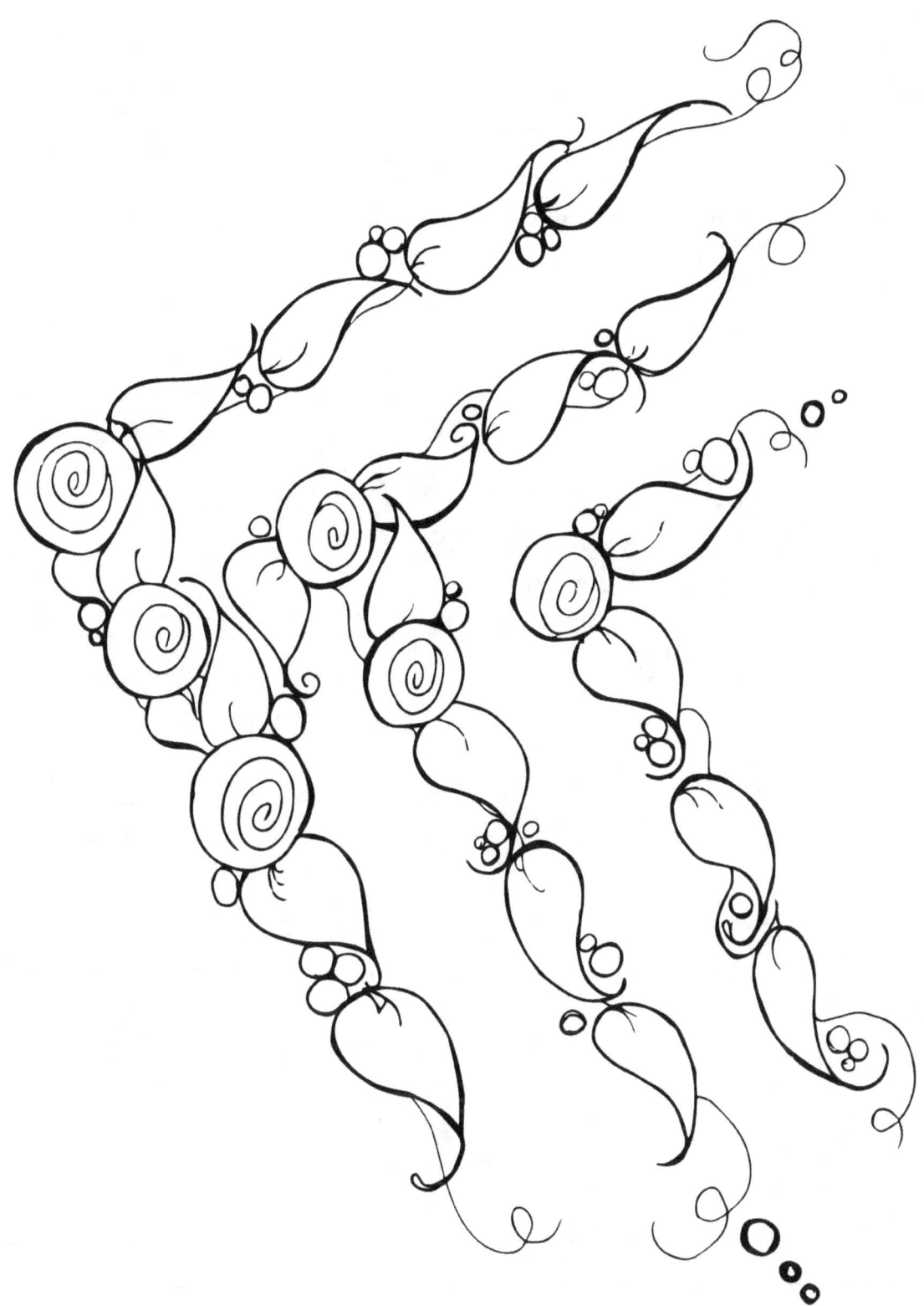

Morning thoughts:

_____

_____

_____

_____

_____

_____

_____

DATE:

_____

Food

Water: IIII IIII IIII

<u>Breakfast:</u>

_____

_____

_____

_____

Goals & Intentions for today

1

2

3

4

5

6

<u>Lunch:</u>

_____

_____

_____

<u>Dinner:</u>

_____

_____

_____

_____

GRATITUDE

<u>Snacks:</u>

_____

_____

_____

<u>Notes:</u>

_____

_____

_____

REFLECTION

_____

_____

_____

_____

_____

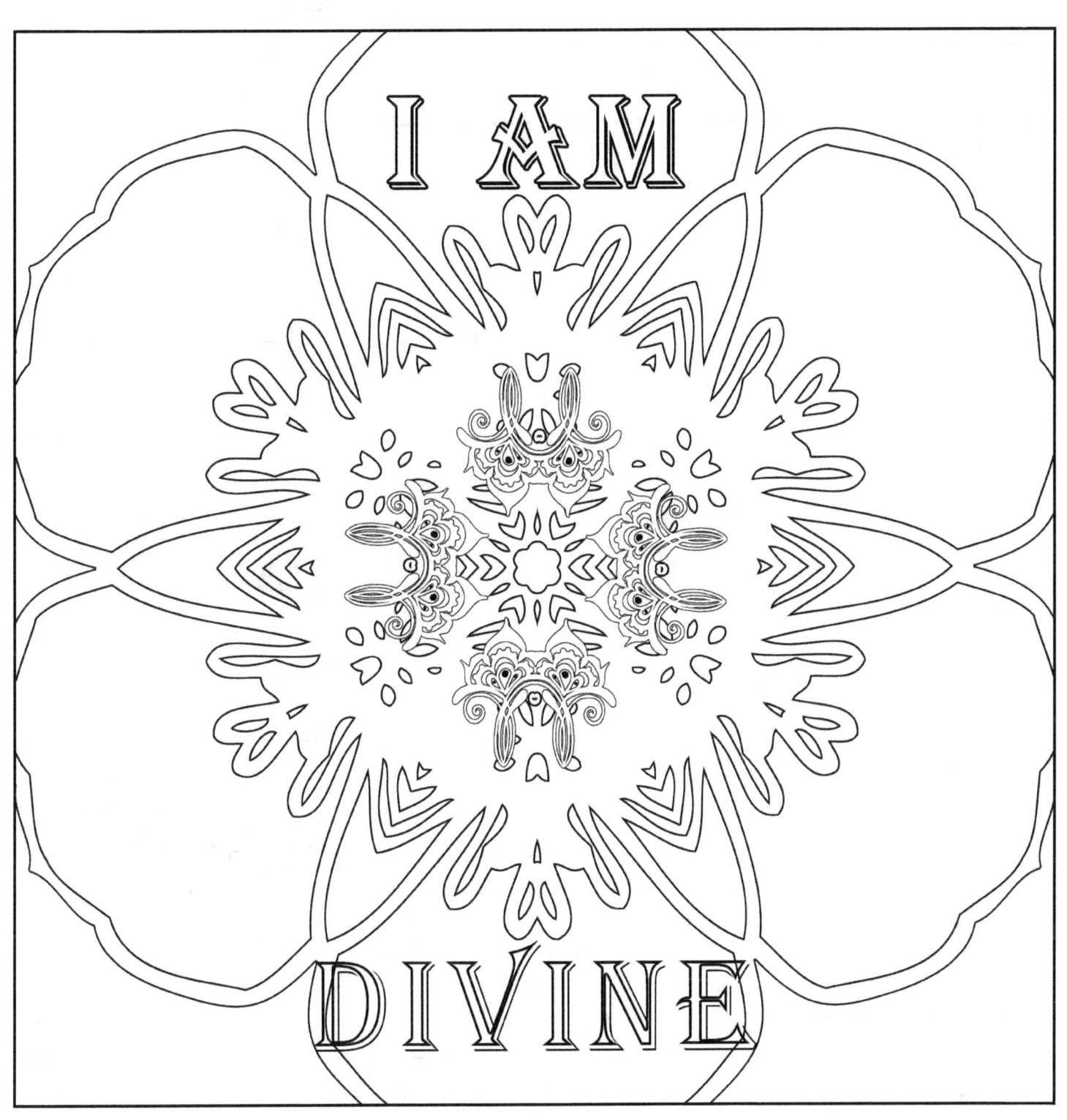

Morning thoughts:

_____
_____
_____
_____
_____
_____

DATE:
_____

Food

Water: IIII IIII IIII

Breakfast:
_____
_____
_____
_____

Goals & Intentions for today

1

2

3

4

5

6

Lunch:
_____
_____
_____
_____

Dinner:
_____
_____
_____
_____

GRATITUDE

Snacks:
_____
_____

Notes:
_____
_____
_____

REFLECTION

_____
_____
_____
_____
_____

Morning thoughts:
_____
_____
_____
_____
_____
_____

DATE:
_____

Goals & Intentions for today

1
2
3
4
5
6

GRATITUDE

Food

Water: IIII IIII IIII

Breakfast:
_____
_____
_____
_____

Lunch:
_____
_____
_____
_____

Dinner:
_____
_____
_____
_____

Snacks:
_____
_____

Notes:
_____
_____
_____

REFLECTION

_____
_____
_____
_____
_____

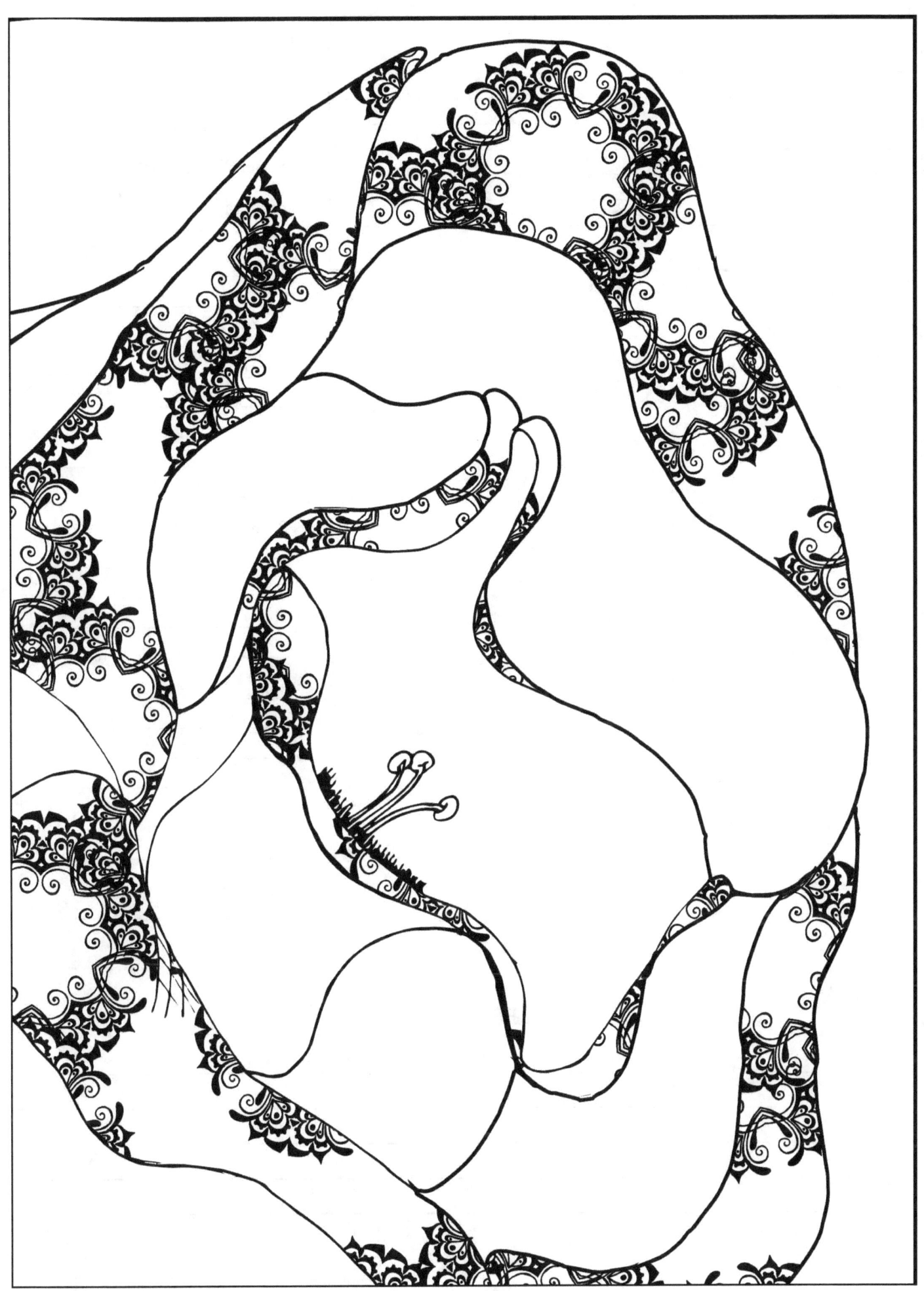

Morning thoughts:

_____
_____
_____
_____
_____
_____
_____

DATE:
_____

Food

Water: IIII IIII IIII

<u>Breakfast:</u>
_____
_____
_____
_____

<u>Lunch:</u>
_____
_____
_____
_____

<u>Dinner:</u>
_____
_____
_____
_____

<u>Snacks:</u>
_____
_____

<u>Notes:</u>
_____
_____
_____

Goals & Intentions for today

1

2

3

4

5

6

GRATITUDE

REFLECTION

_____
_____
_____
_____
_____

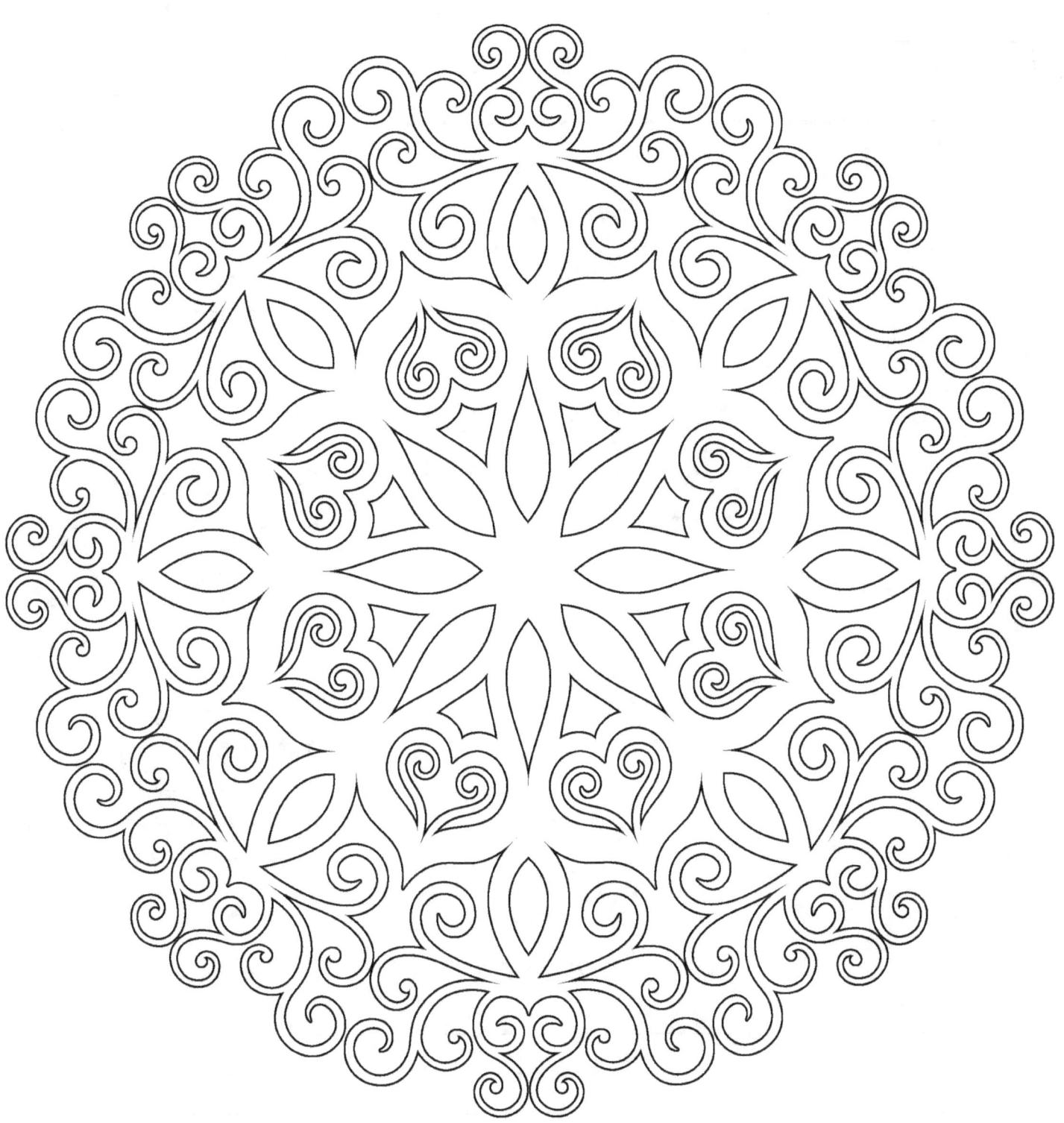

Morning thoughts:

_____
_____
_____
_____
_____
_____
_____

DATE: _____

Food

Water: IIII IIII IIII

<u>Breakfast:</u>

_____
_____
_____
_____

Goals & Intentions for today

1

2

3

4

5

6

<u>Lunch:</u>

_____
_____
_____
_____

<u>Dinner:</u>

_____
_____
_____
_____

GRATITUDE

<u>Snacks:</u>

_____
_____

<u>Notes:</u>

_____
_____
_____

REFLECTION

_____
_____
_____
_____
_____

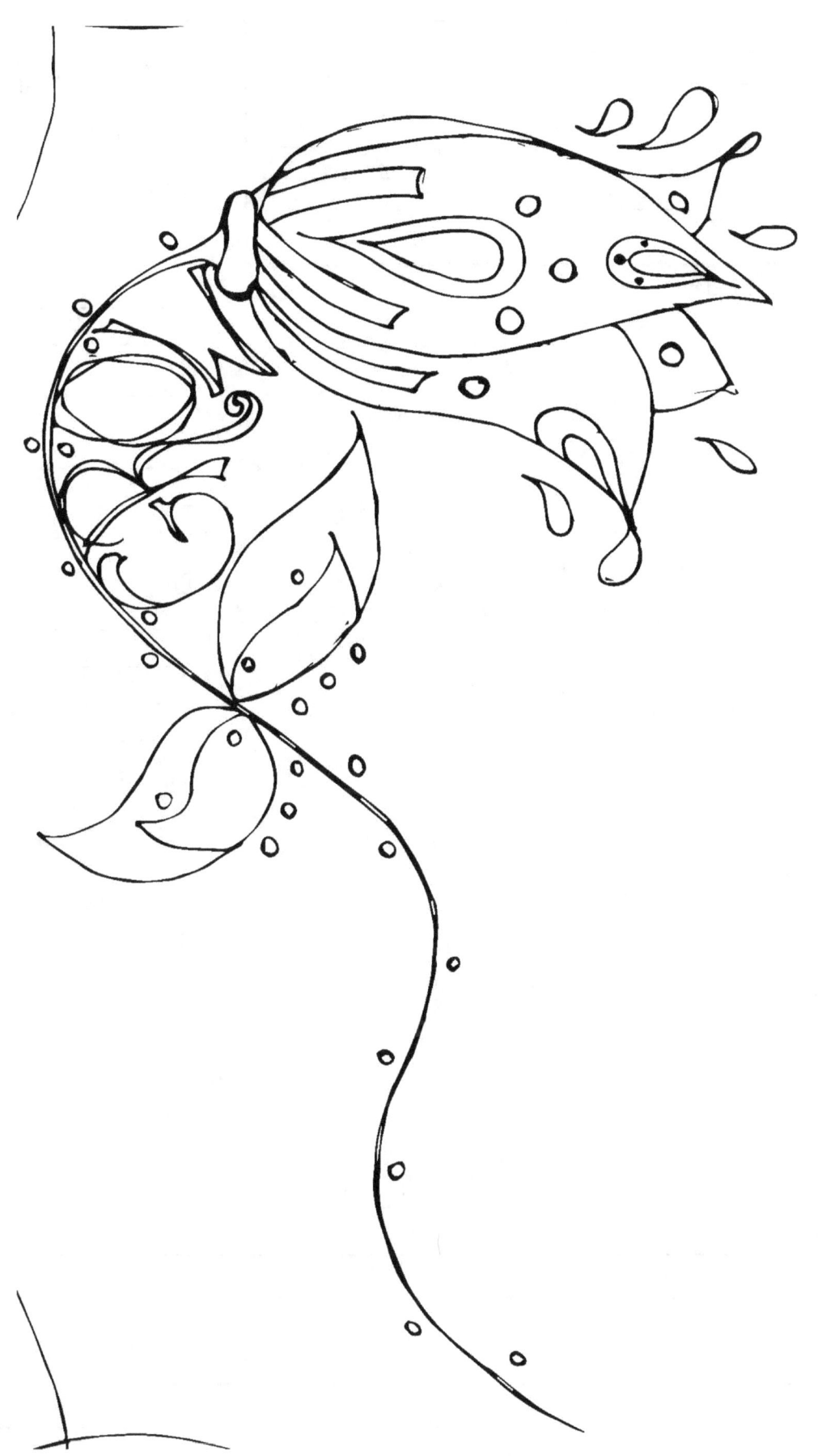

Morning thoughts:
_____
_____
_____
_____
_____
_____
_____

DATE: _____

Food

Water: IIII IIII IIII

Breakfast:
_____
_____
_____
_____

Lunch:
_____
_____
_____

Dinner:
_____
_____
_____

Snacks:
_____
_____

Notes:
_____
_____
_____

Goals & Intentions for today

1
2
3
4
5
6

GRATITUDE

REFLECTION

_____
_____
_____
_____
_____

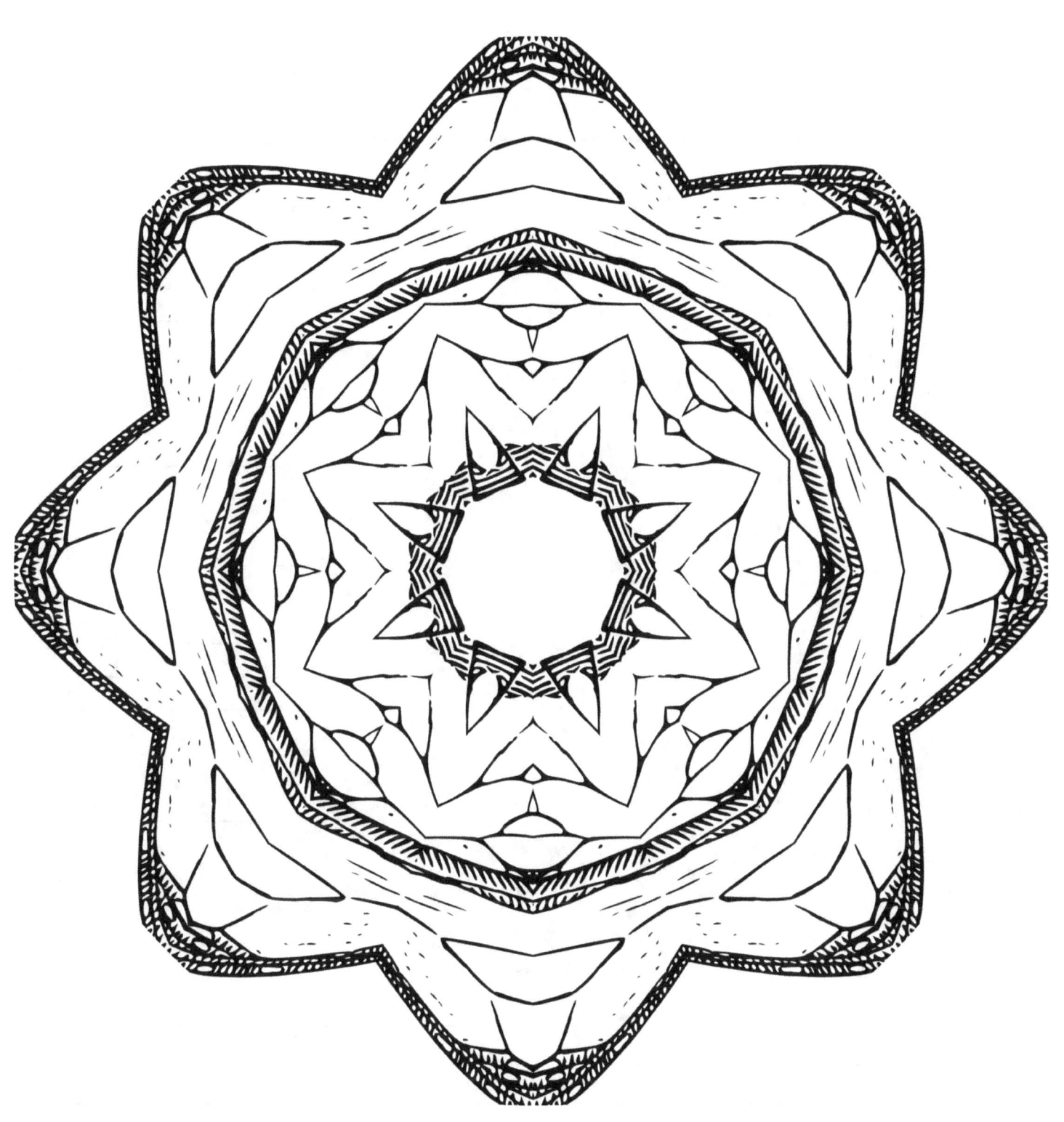

Morning thoughts:

_____
_____
_____
_____
_____
_____
_____

DATE: _____

Food

Water: IIII IIII IIII

Breakfast:
_____
_____
_____
_____

Lunch:
_____
_____
_____
_____

Dinner:
_____
_____
_____
_____

Snacks:
_____
_____

Notes:
_____
_____
_____

Goals & Intentions for today

1
2
3
4
5
6

GRATITUDE

REFLECTION

_____
_____
_____
_____
_____

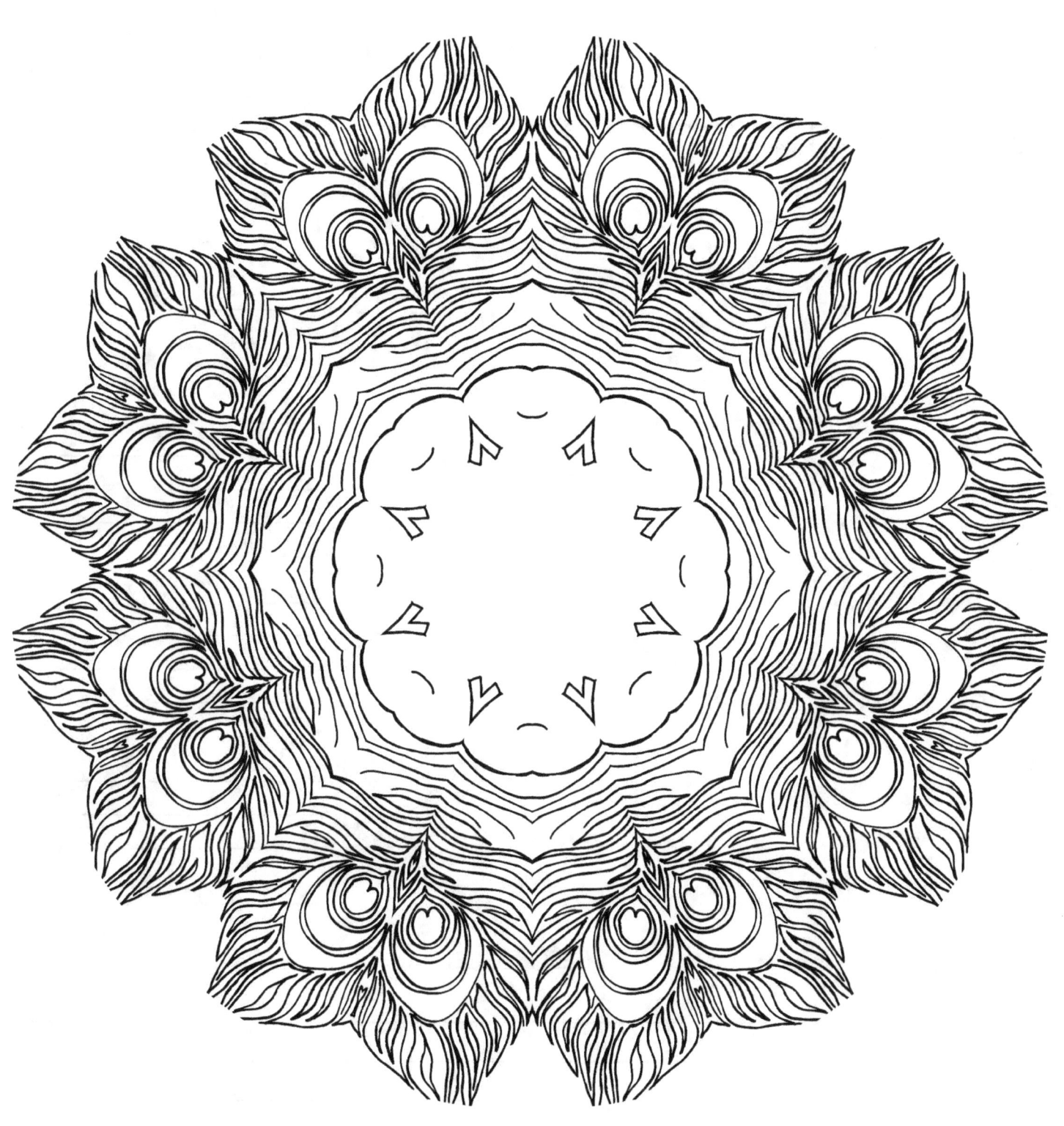

Morning thoughts:

_____
_____
_____
_____
_____
_____
_____

DATE:

_____

Goals & Intentions for today

1

2

3

4

5

6

GRATITUDE

Food

Water: IIII IIII IIII

Breakfast:

_____
_____
_____
_____

Lunch:

_____
_____
_____

Dinner:

_____
_____
_____

Snacks:

_____
_____

Notes:

_____
_____
_____

REFLECTION

_____
_____
_____
_____
_____

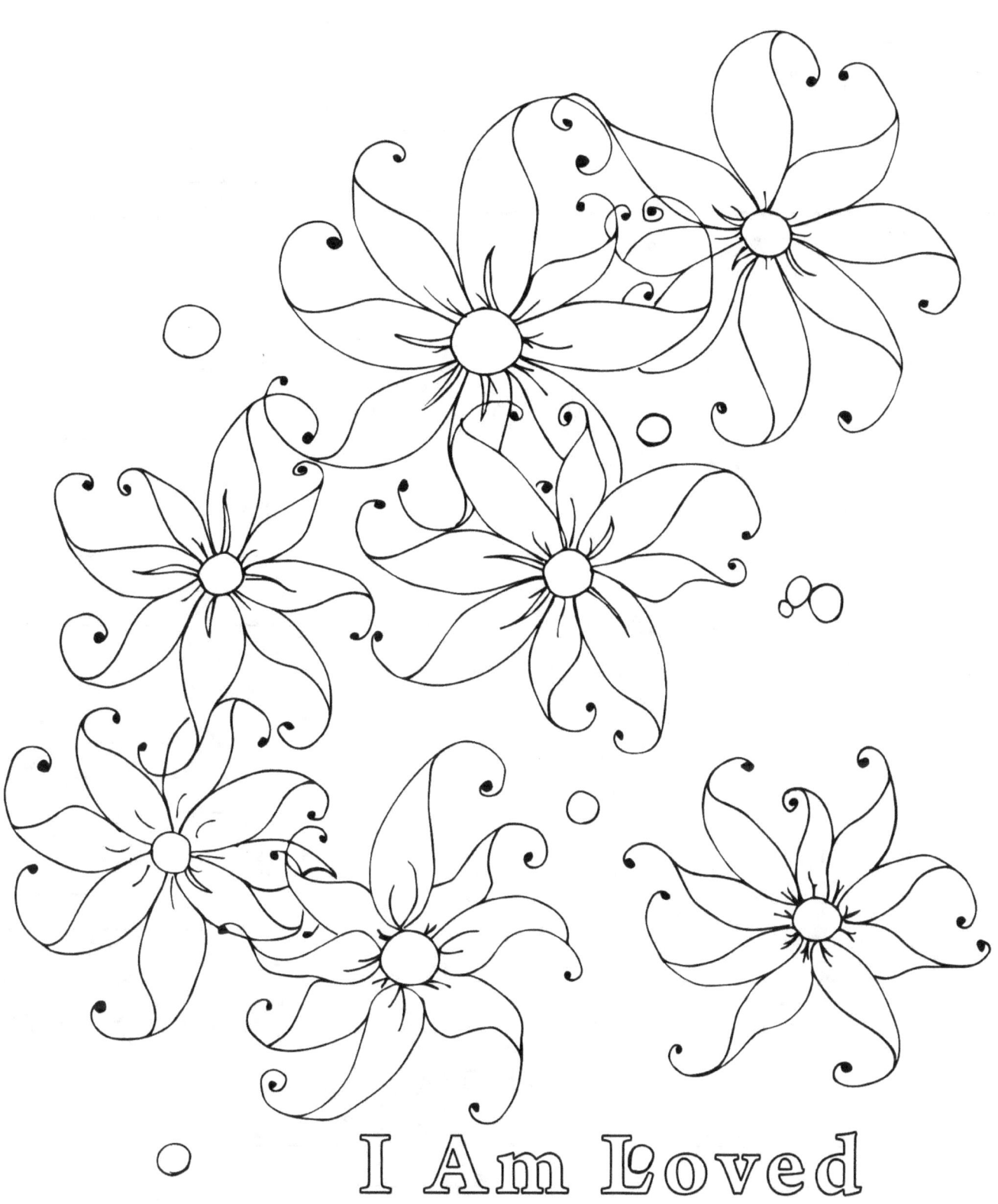

I Am Loved

Morning thoughts:

_____
_____
_____
_____
_____
_____
_____

DATE: _____

Food

Water: IIII IIII IIII

Breakfast:

_____
_____
_____
_____

Lunch:

_____
_____
_____
_____

Dinner:

_____
_____
_____
_____

Snacks:

_____
_____

Notes:

_____
_____
_____

Goals & Intentions for today

1
2
3
4
5
6

GRATITUDE

REFLECTION

_____
_____
_____
_____
_____

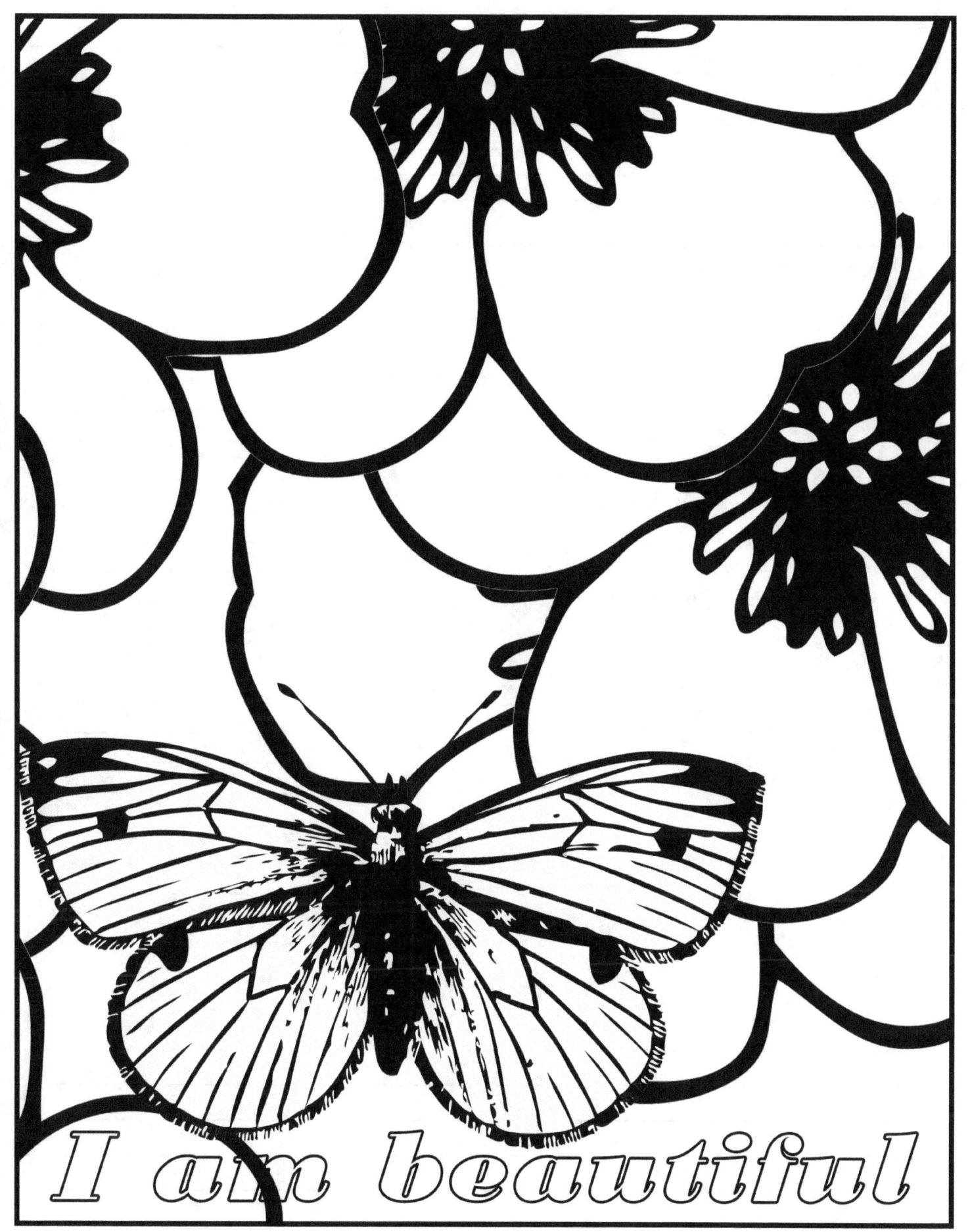

Morning thoughts:

_____
_____
_____
_____
_____
_____
_____

DATE:

_____

Food

Water: IIII IIII IIII

<u>Breakfast:</u>

_____
_____
_____
_____

<u>Lunch:</u>

_____
_____
_____
_____

<u>Dinner:</u>

_____
_____
_____
_____

<u>Snacks:</u>

_____
_____

<u>Notes:</u>

_____
_____
_____

Goals & Intentions for today

1

2

3

4

5

6

GRATITUDE

REFLECTION

_____
_____
_____
_____
_____

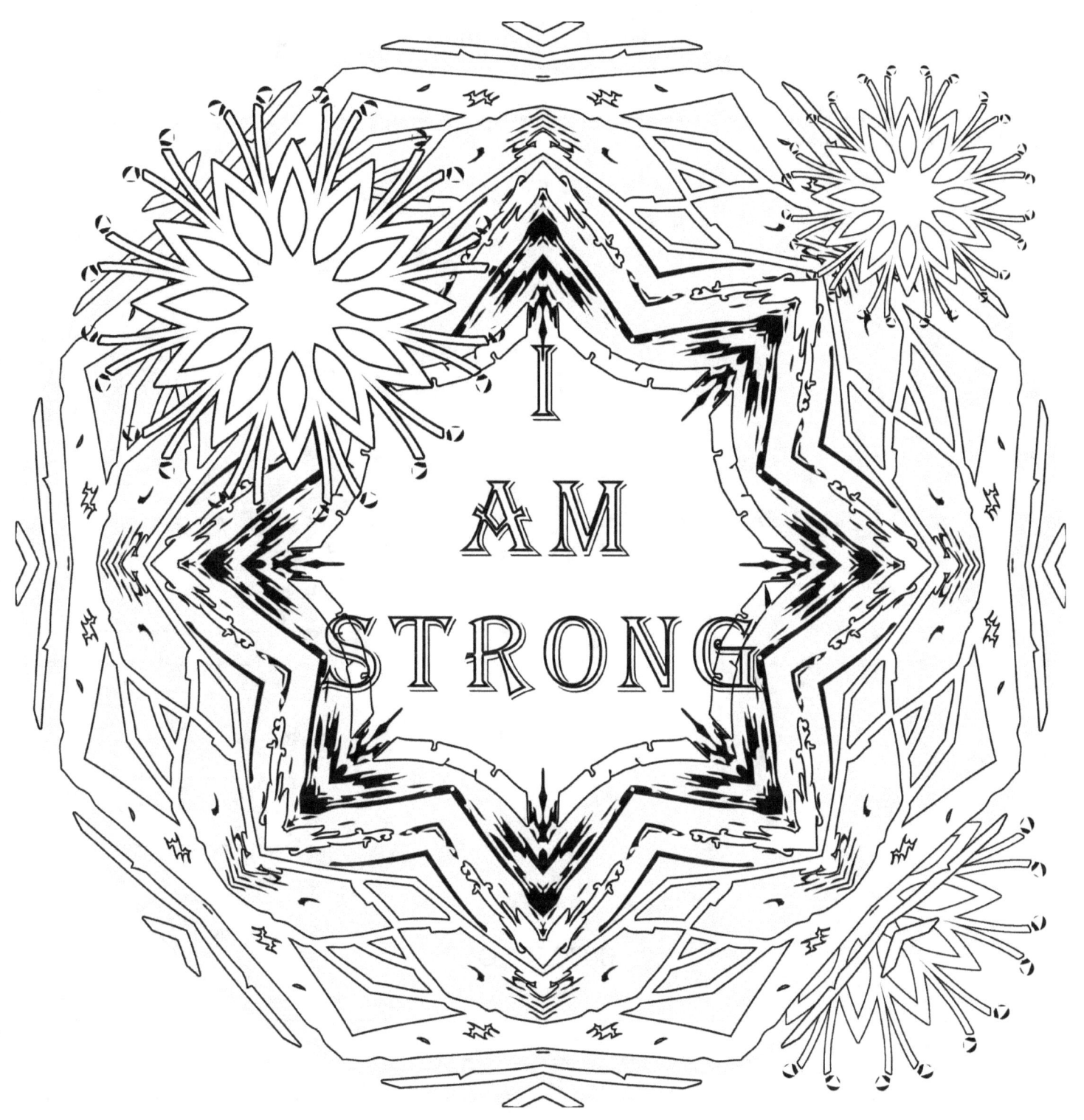

Morning thoughts:

_____
_____
_____
_____
_____
_____
_____

DATE:
_____

Food

Water: IIII IIII IIII

<u>Breakfast:</u>
_____
_____
_____
_____

<u>Lunch:</u>
_____
_____
_____
_____

<u>Dinner:</u>
_____
_____
_____
_____

<u>Snacks:</u>
_____
_____

<u>Notes:</u>
_____
_____
_____

Goals & Intentions for today

1
2
3
4
5
6

GRATITUDE

REFLECTION

_____
_____
_____
_____
_____

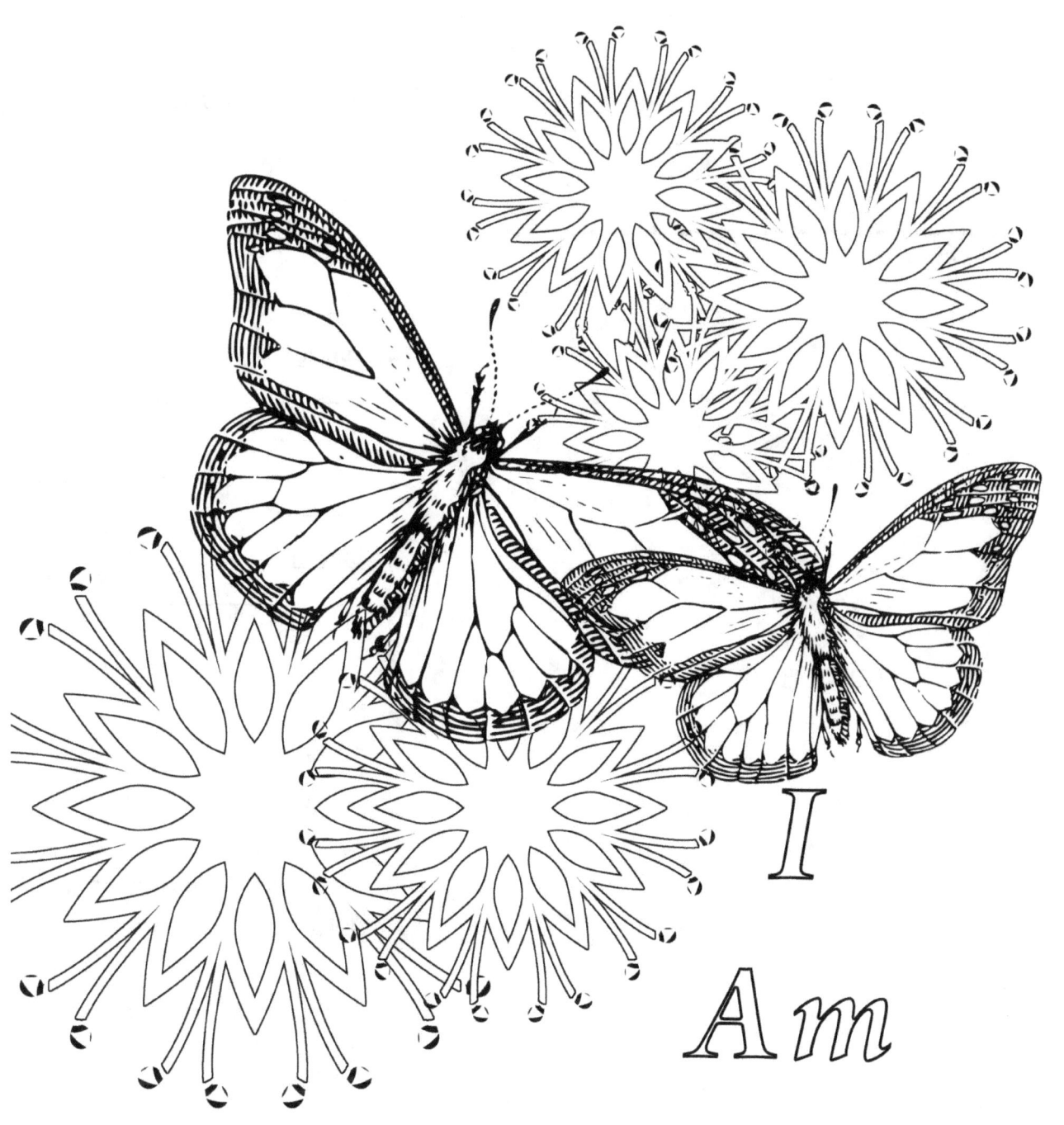

I

Am

Grateful

Morning thoughts:

_____
_____
_____
_____
_____
_____

DATE:
_____

Food

Water: IIII IIII IIII

<u>Breakfast:</u>
_____
_____
_____
_____

<u>Lunch:</u>
_____
_____
_____
_____

<u>Dinner:</u>
_____
_____
_____
_____

<u>Snacks:</u>
_____
_____

<u>Notes:</u>
_____
_____
_____

Goals & Intentions for today

1

2

3

4

5

6

GRATITUDE

REFLECTION

_____
_____
_____
_____
_____

I Am Perfect
As I Am

Morning thoughts:

_____
_____
_____
_____
_____
_____
_____

DATE:

_____

Food

Water: IIII IIII IIII

Breakfast:

_____
_____
_____
_____

Goals & Intentions for today

1

2

3

4

5

6

Lunch:

_____
_____
_____
_____

Dinner:

_____
_____
_____
_____

GRATITUDE

Snacks:

_____
_____

Notes:

_____
_____
_____

REFLECTION

_____
_____
_____
_____
_____

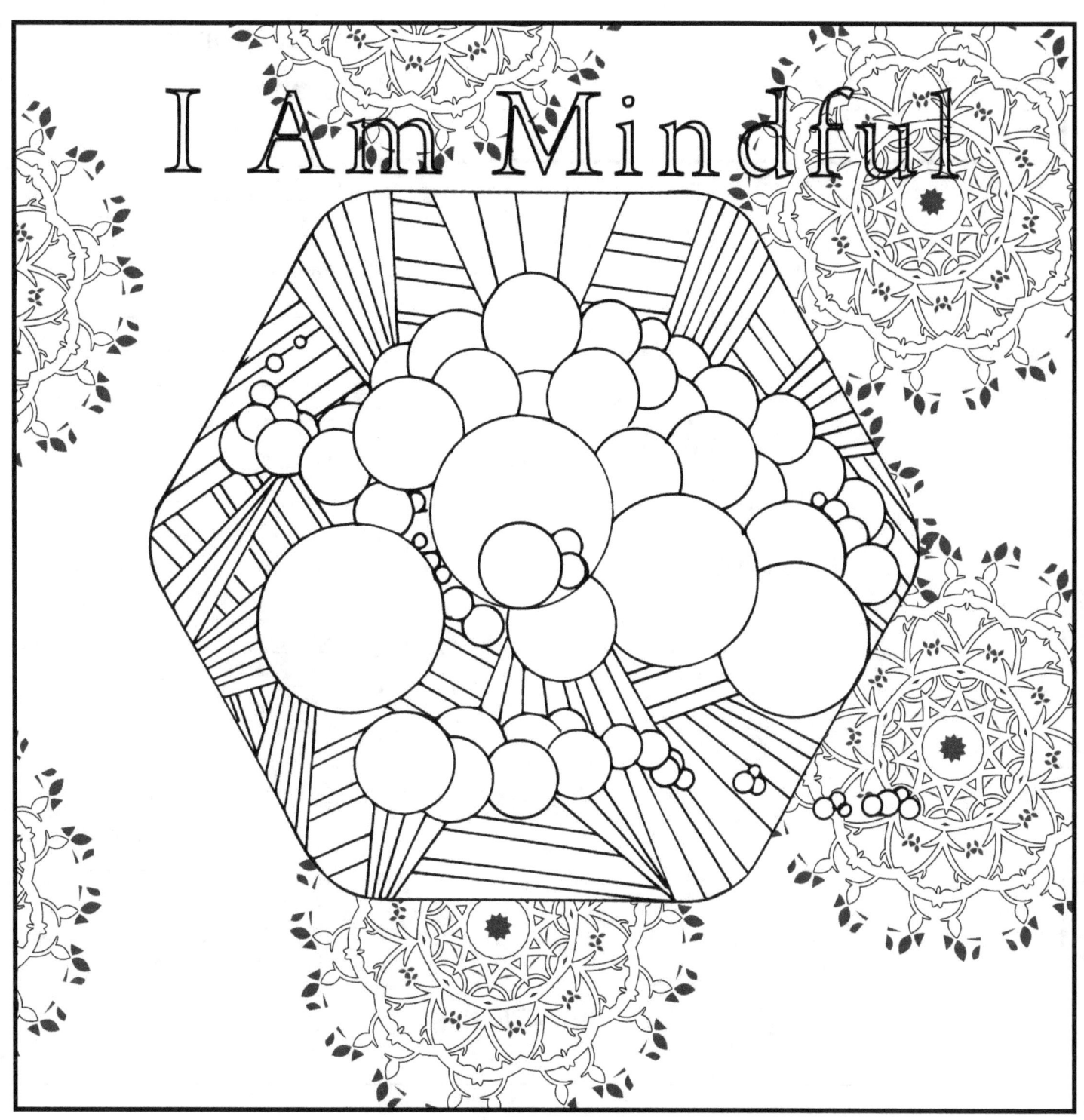

Morning thoughts:

_____
_____
_____
_____
_____
_____
_____

DATE: _____

Food

Water: IIII IIII IIII

Breakfast:
_____
_____
_____
_____

Lunch:
_____
_____
_____

Dinner:
_____
_____
_____
_____

Snacks:
_____
_____

Notes:
_____
_____
_____

Goals & Intentions for today

1

2

3

4

5

6

GRATITUDE

REFLECTION

_____
_____
_____
_____
_____

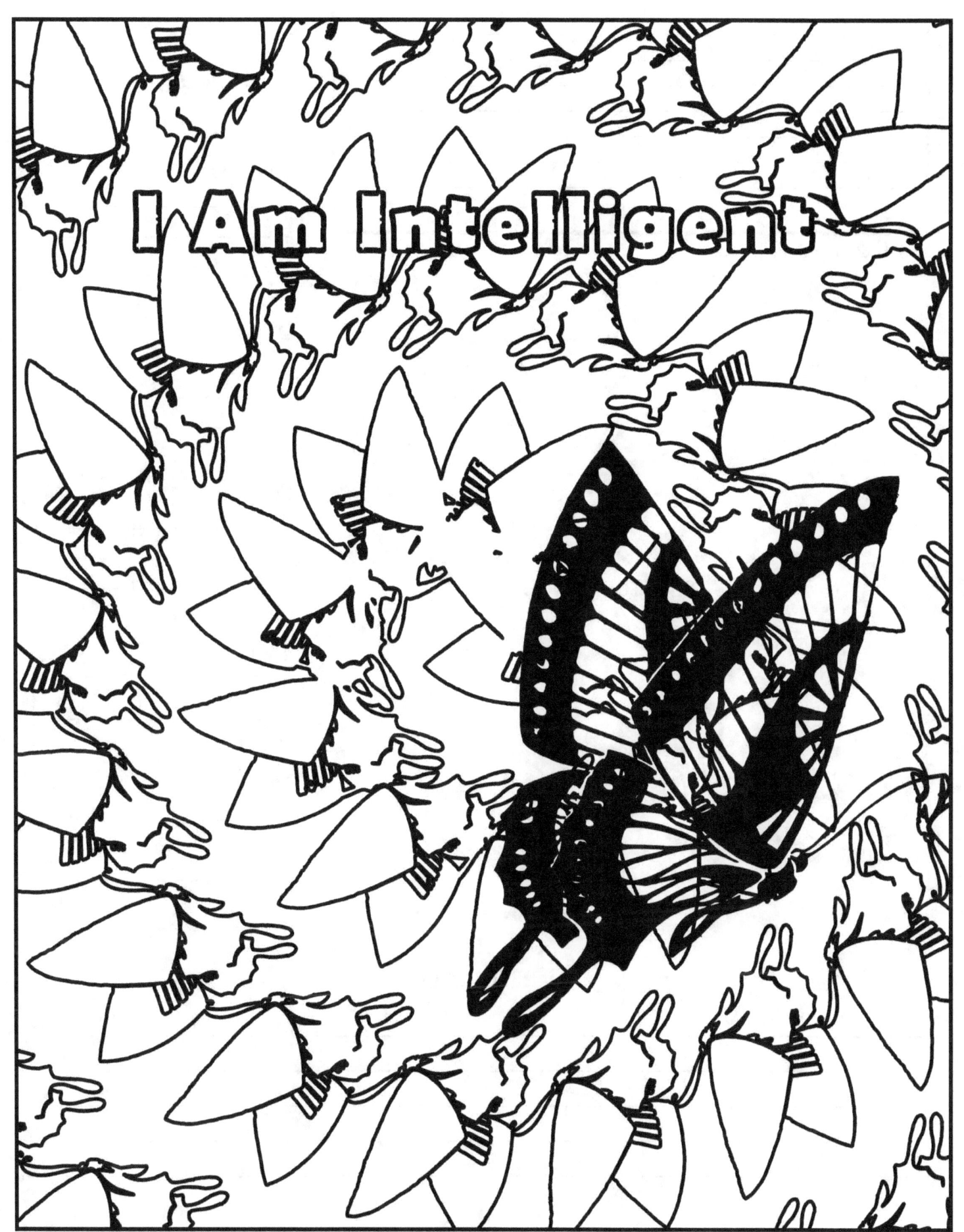

Morning thoughts:
_____
_____
_____
_____
_____
_____
_____

DATE: _____

Goals & Intentions for today

1

2

3

4

5

6

GRATITUDE

Food

Water: IIII IIII IIII

<u>Breakfast:</u>
_____
_____
_____
_____

<u>Lunch:</u>
_____
_____
_____
_____

<u>Dinner:</u>
_____
_____
_____
_____

<u>Snacks:</u>
_____
_____

<u>Notes:</u>
_____
_____
_____

REFLECTION

_____
_____
_____
_____
_____

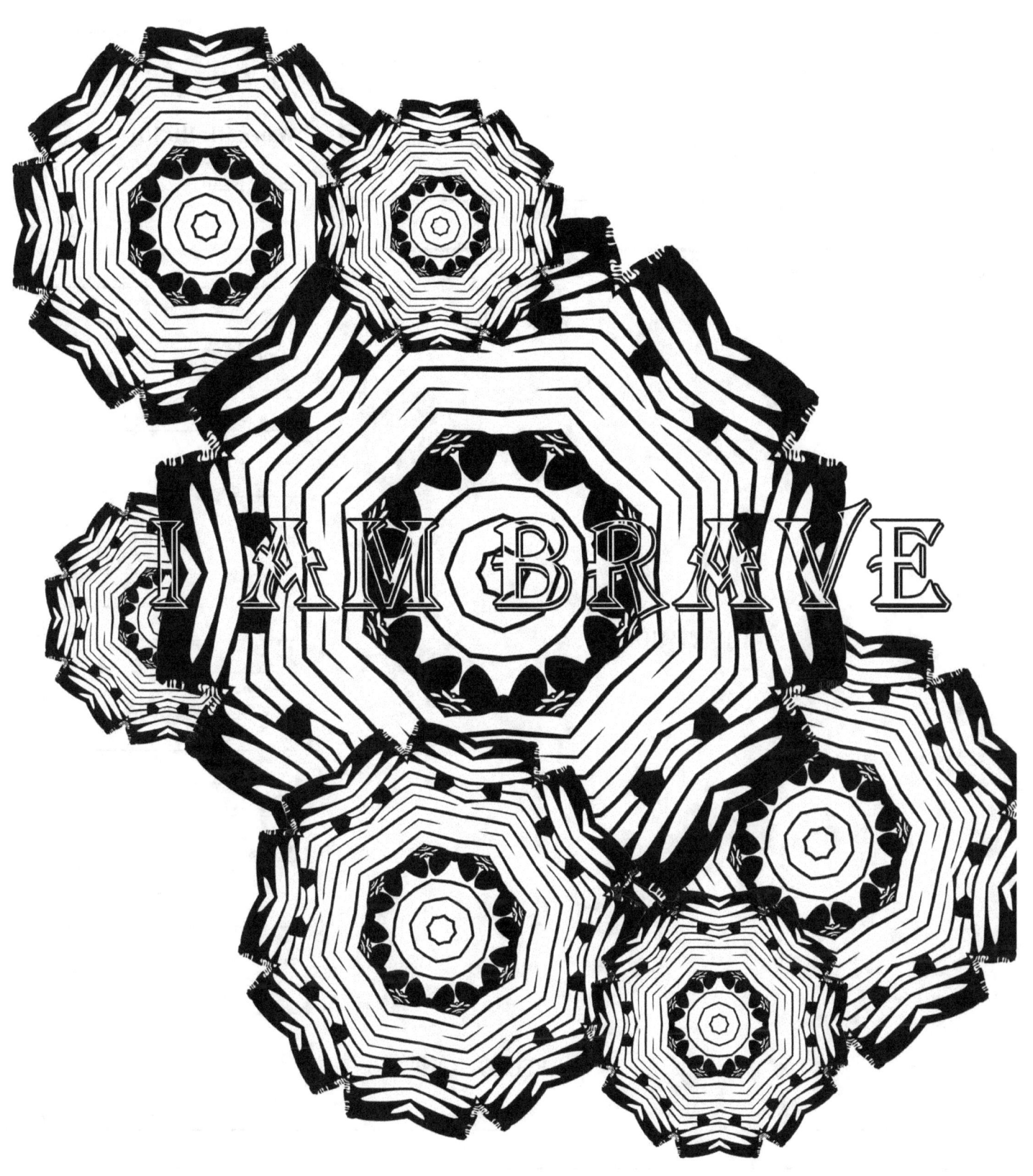

Morning thoughts:

_____
_____
_____
_____
_____
_____
_____

Goals & Intentions for today

1

2

3

4

5

6

GRATITUDE

Food

Water: IIII IIII IIII

<u>Breakfast:</u>

_____
_____
_____
_____

<u>Lunch:</u>

_____
_____
_____
_____

<u>Dinner:</u>

_____
_____
_____
_____

<u>Snacks:</u>

_____
_____

<u>Notes:</u>

_____
_____
_____

REFLECTION

_____
_____
_____
_____
_____

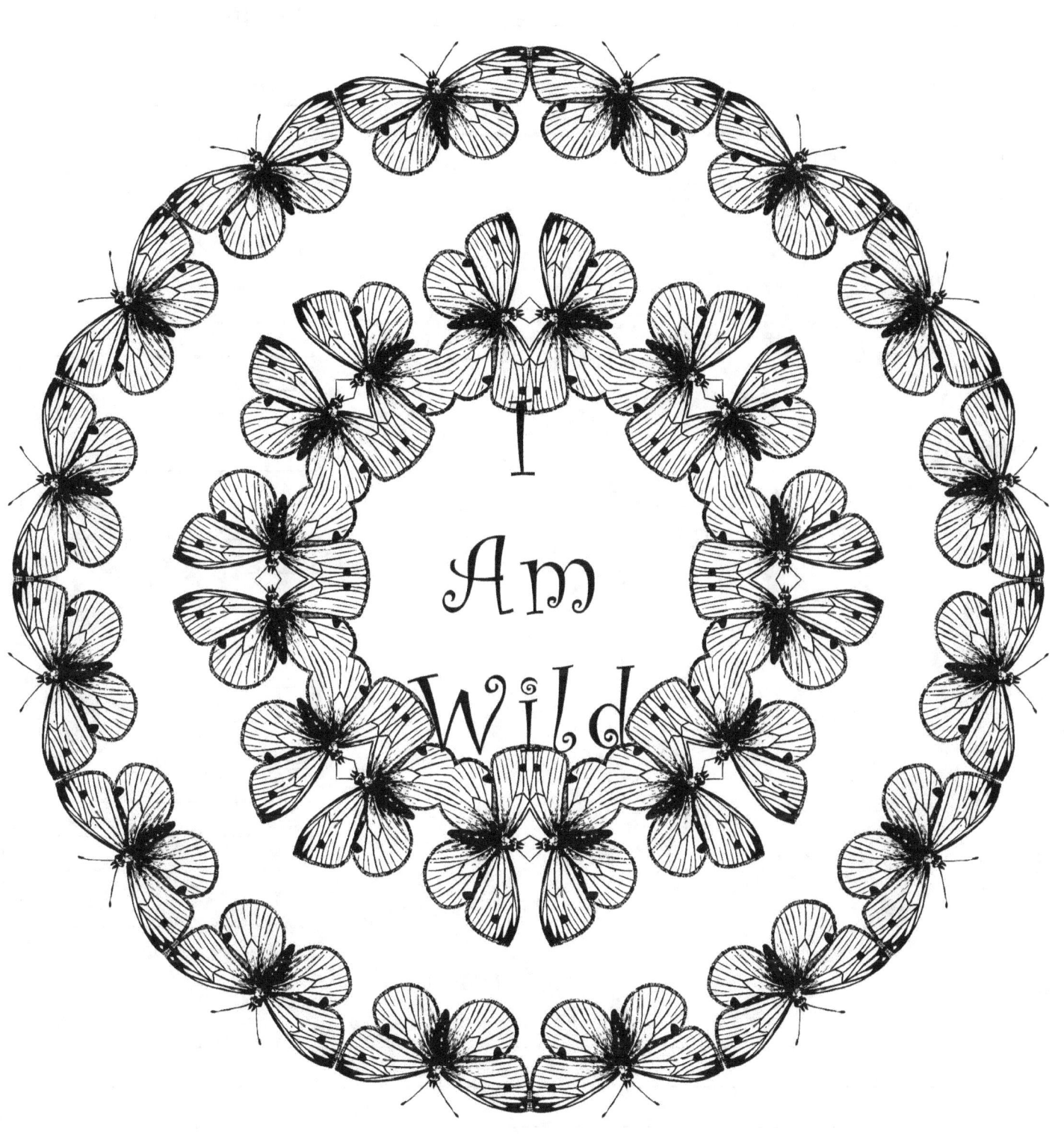

Morning thoughts:
_____
_____
_____
_____
_____
_____
_____

DATE:
_____

Food

Water: IIII IIII IIII

Breakfast:
_____
_____
_____
_____

Goals & Intentions for today

1

2

3

4

5

6

Lunch:
_____
_____
_____
_____

Dinner:
_____
_____
_____
_____

GRATITUDE

Snacks:
_____
_____

Notes:
_____
_____
_____

REFLECTION

_____
_____
_____
_____
_____

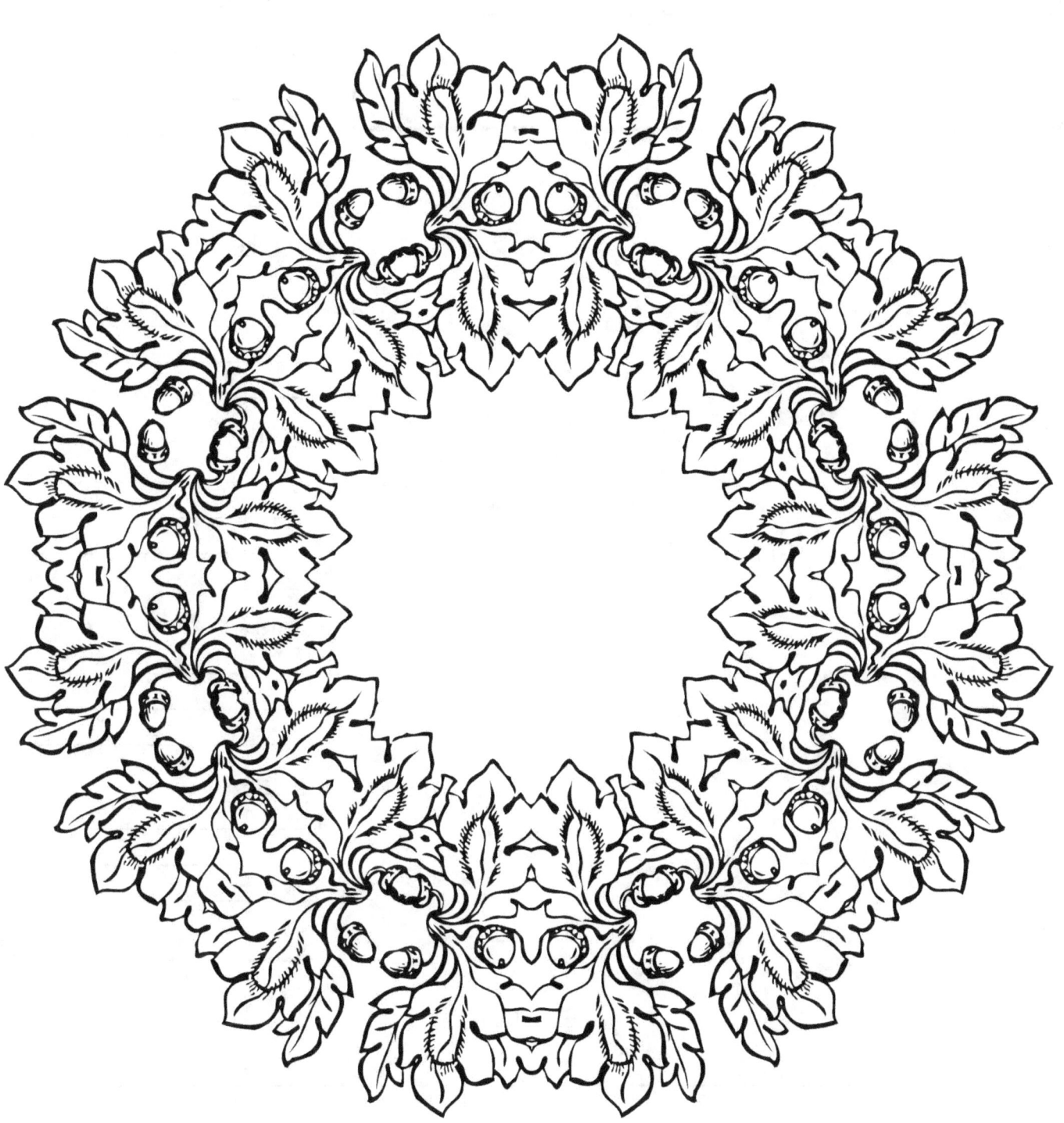

Morning thoughts:

_____
_____
_____
_____
_____
_____

DATE:

_____

Food

Water: IIII IIII IIII

Breakfast:

_____
_____
_____
_____

Lunch:

_____
_____
_____
_____

Dinner:

_____
_____
_____

Snacks:

_____
_____

Notes:

_____
_____
_____

Goals & Intentions for today

1
2
3
4
5
6

GRATITUDE

REFLECTION

_____
_____
_____
_____
_____

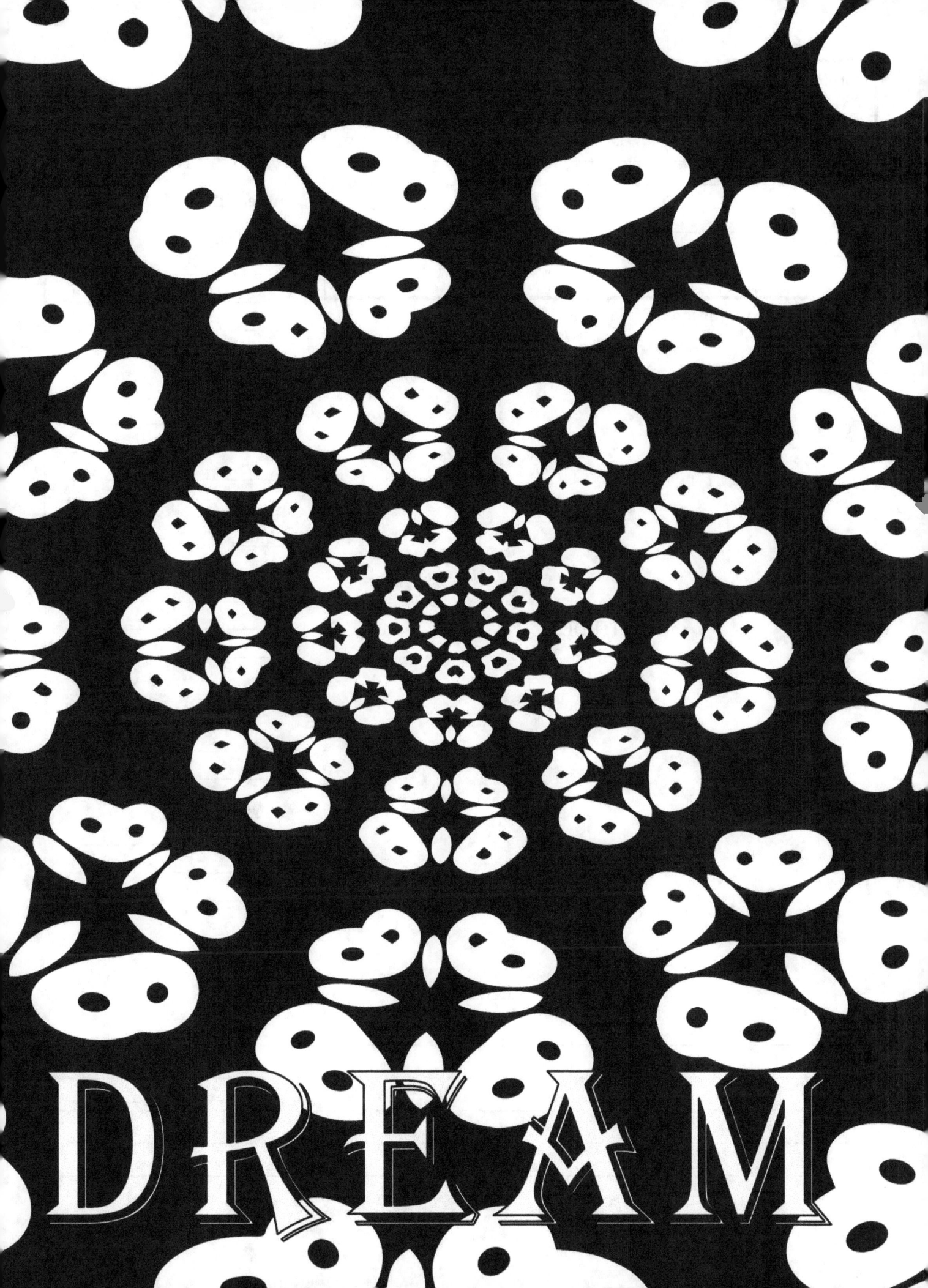

Morning thoughts:

_____
_____
_____
_____
_____
_____

DATE: _____

Food

Water: IIII IIII IIII

Breakfast:

_____
_____
_____
_____

Lunch:

_____
_____
_____
_____

Dinner:

_____
_____
_____
_____

Snacks:

_____
_____

Notes:

_____
_____
_____

Goals & Intentions for today

1
2
3
4
5
6

GRATITUDE

REFLECTION

_____
_____
_____
_____

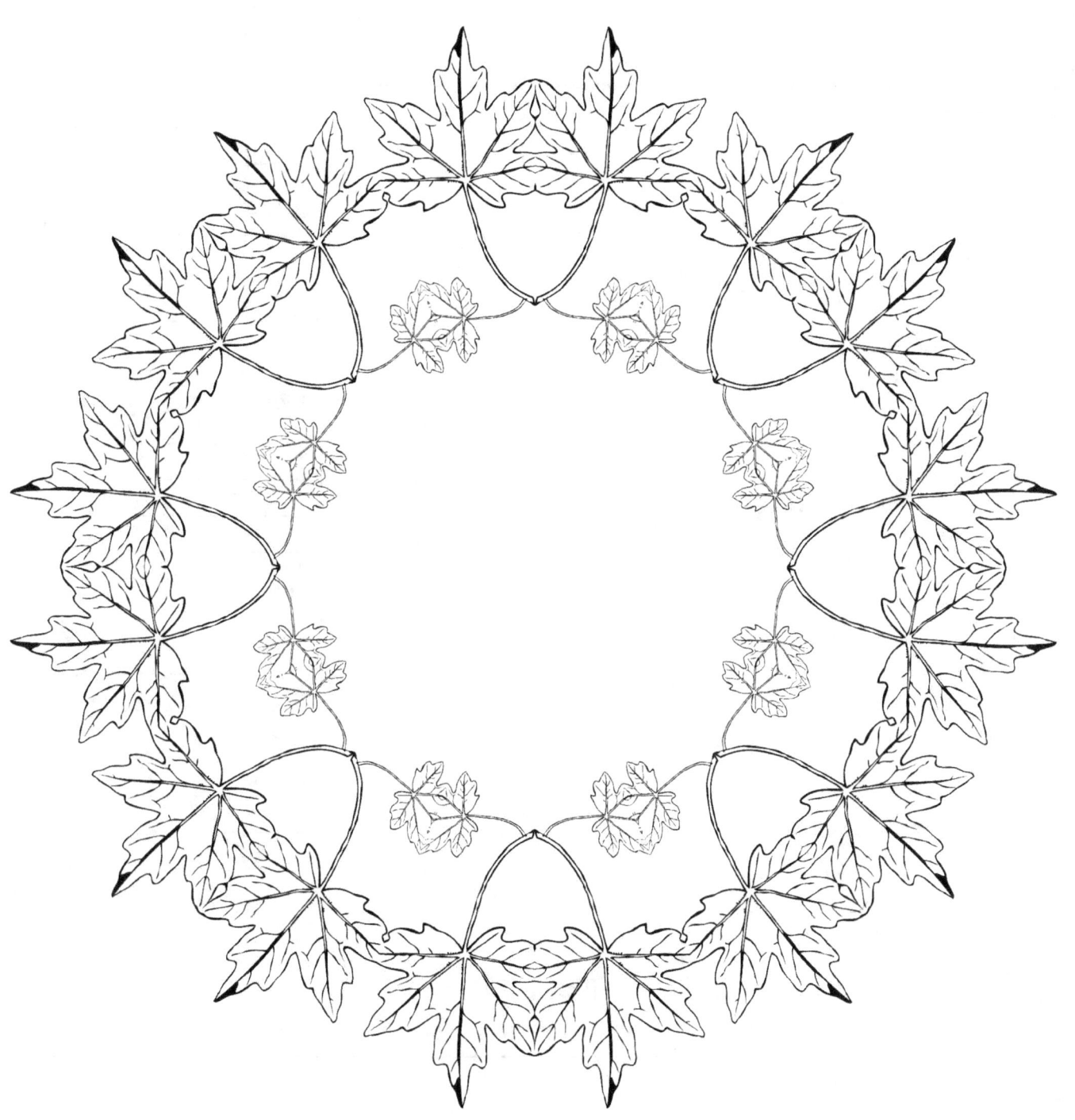

Morning thoughts:

_____
_____
_____
_____
_____
_____
_____

DATE: _____

Goals & Intentions for today

1

2

3

4

5

6

GRATITUDE

Food

Water: IIII IIII IIII

Breakfast:

_____
_____
_____
_____

Lunch:

_____
_____
_____
_____

Dinner:

_____
_____
_____
_____

Snacks:

_____
_____
_____

Notes:

_____
_____
_____

REFLECTION

_____
_____
_____
_____
_____

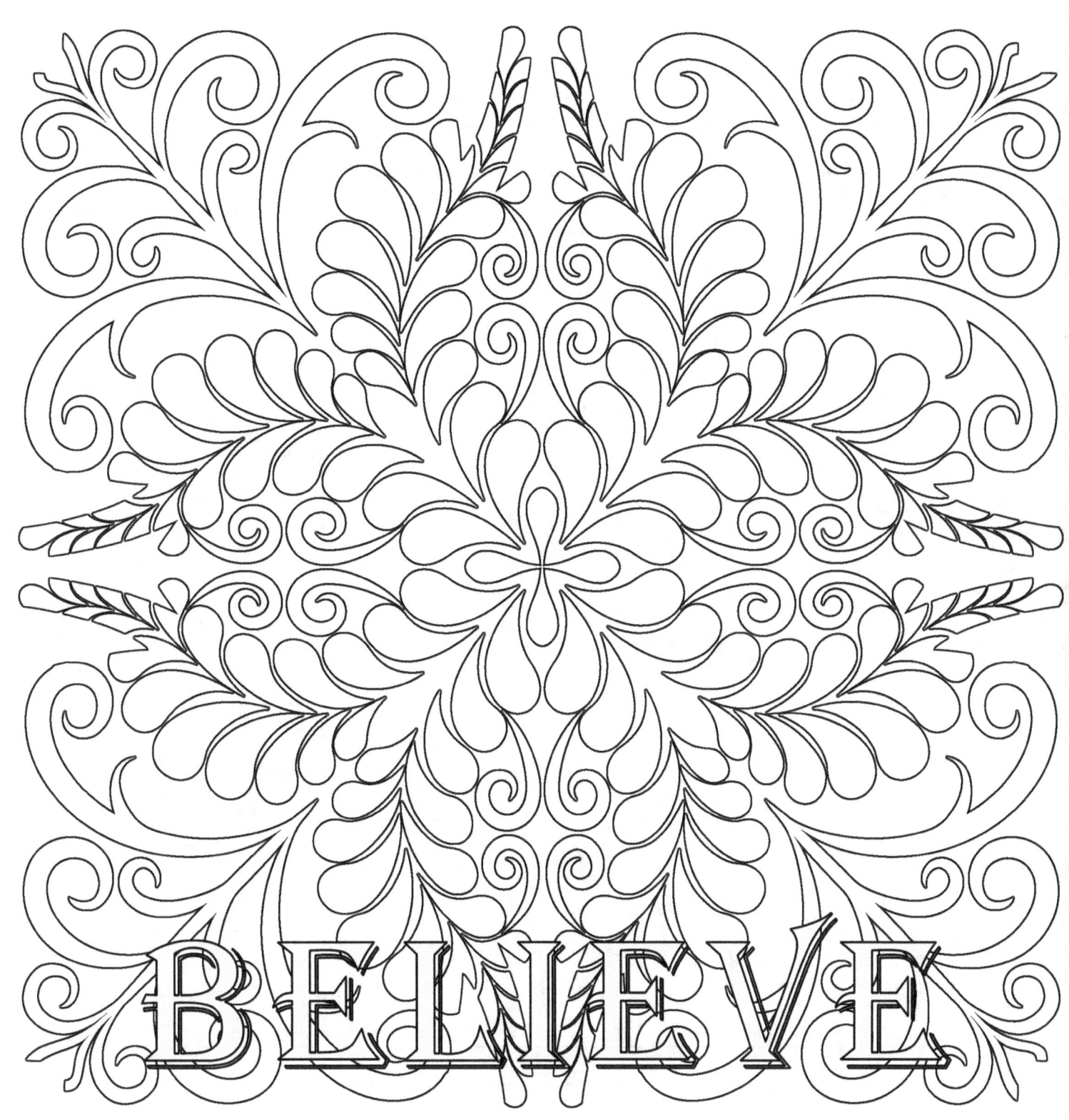

Morning thoughts:
_____
_____
_____
_____
_____
_____
_____

DATE:
_____

Food

Water: IIII IIII IIII

Breakfast:
_____
_____
_____
_____

Goals & Intentions for today

1
2
3
4
5
6

Lunch:
_____
_____
_____

GRATITUDE

Dinner:
_____
_____
_____
_____

Snacks:
_____
_____

Notes:
_____
_____
_____
_____

REFLECTION

_____
_____
_____
_____
_____

Morning thoughts:

_____
_____
_____
_____
_____
_____
_____

DATE:

_____

Food

Water: IIII IIII IIII

Breakfast:

_____
_____
_____
_____

Lunch:

_____
_____
_____
_____

Dinner:

_____
_____
_____

Goals & Intentions for today

1

2

3

4

5

6

Snacks:

_____
_____

Notes:

_____
_____
_____

GRATITUDE

REFLECTION

_____
_____
_____
_____
_____

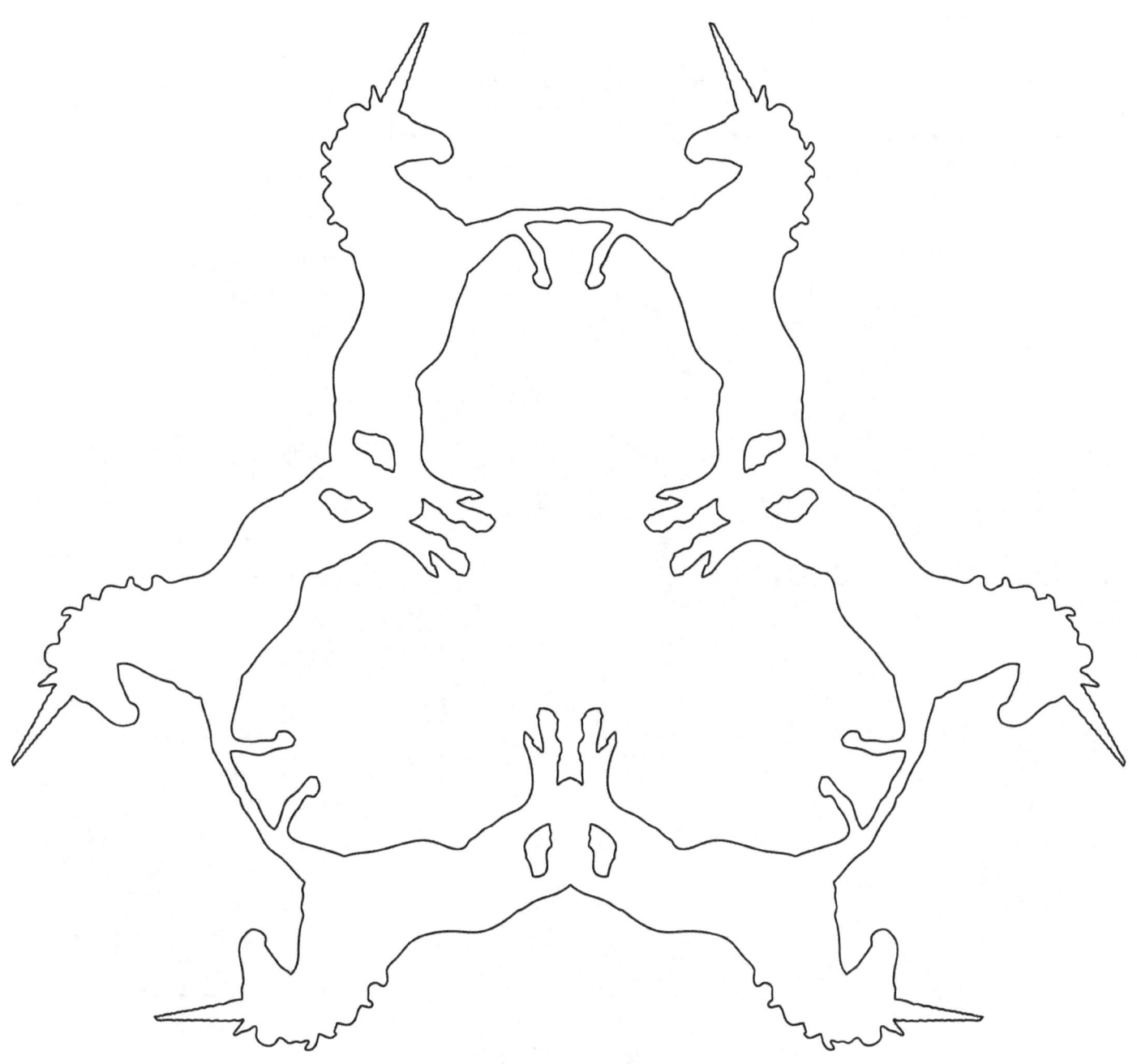

Morning thoughts:

_____
_____
_____
_____
_____
_____
_____

DATE: _____

Food

Water: IIII IIII IIII

Breakfast:
_____
_____
_____
_____

Lunch:
_____
_____
_____
_____

Dinner:
_____
_____
_____
_____

Snacks:
_____
_____

Notes:
_____
_____
_____

Goals & Intentions for today

1
2
3
4
5
6

GRATITUDE

REFLECTION

_____
_____
_____
_____
_____

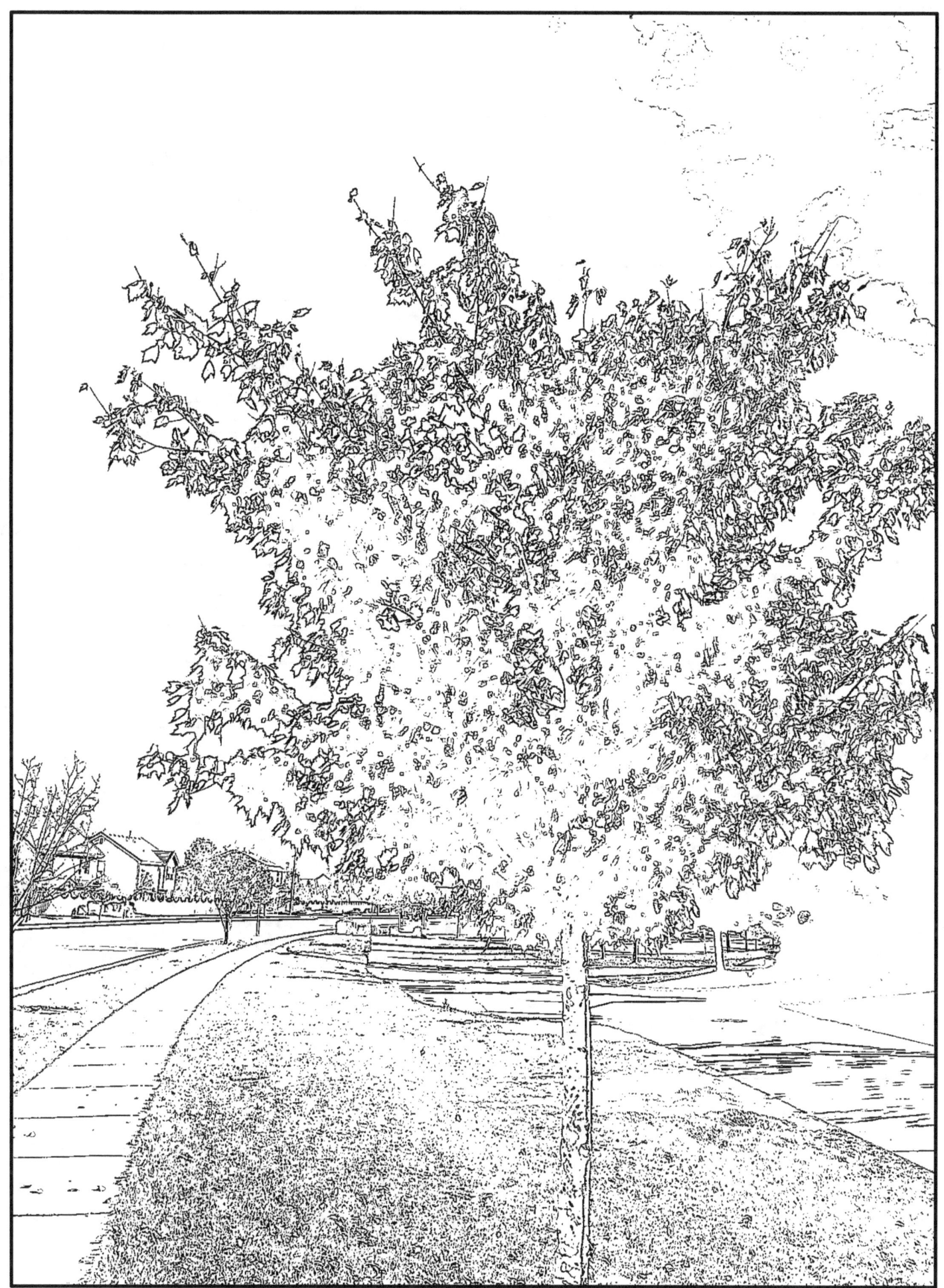

Morning thoughts:

_____
_____
_____
_____
_____
_____
_____

DATE:
_____

Goals & Intentions for today

1

2

3

4

5

6

GRATITUDE

Food

Water: IIII IIII IIII

<u>Breakfast:</u>
_____
_____
_____
_____

<u>Lunch:</u>
_____
_____
_____
_____

<u>Dinner:</u>
_____
_____
_____

<u>Snacks:</u>
_____
_____

<u>Notes:</u>
_____
_____
_____

REFLECTION

_____
_____
_____
_____
_____

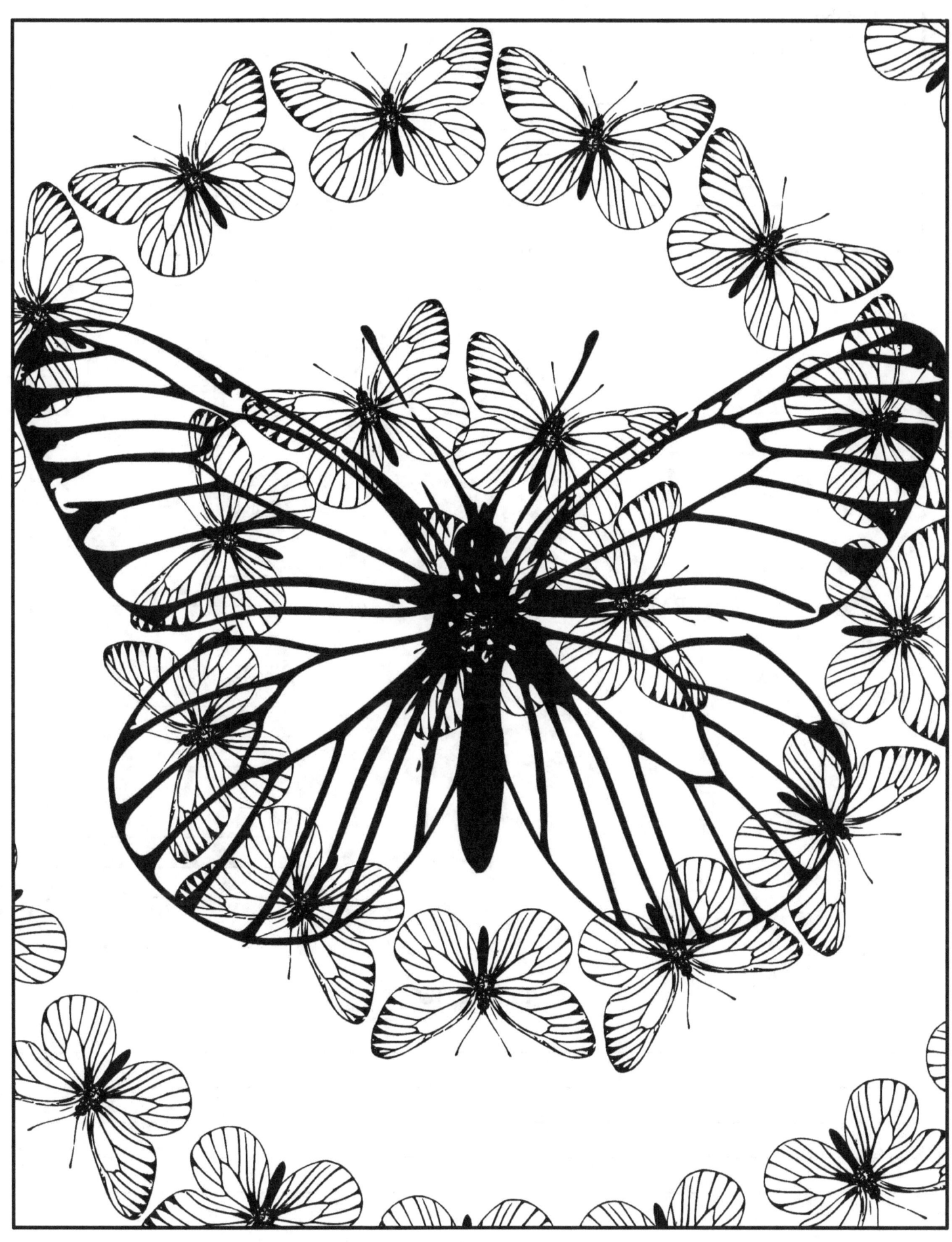

Morning thoughts:

_____
_____
_____
_____
_____
_____

DATE: _____

Food

Water: IIII IIII IIII

Breakfast:

_____
_____
_____
_____

Lunch:

_____
_____
_____
_____

Dinner:

_____
_____
_____
_____

Snacks:

_____
_____
_____

Notes:

_____
_____
_____

Goals & Intentions for today

1
2
3
4
5
6

GRATITUDE

REFLECTION

_____
_____
_____
_____
_____

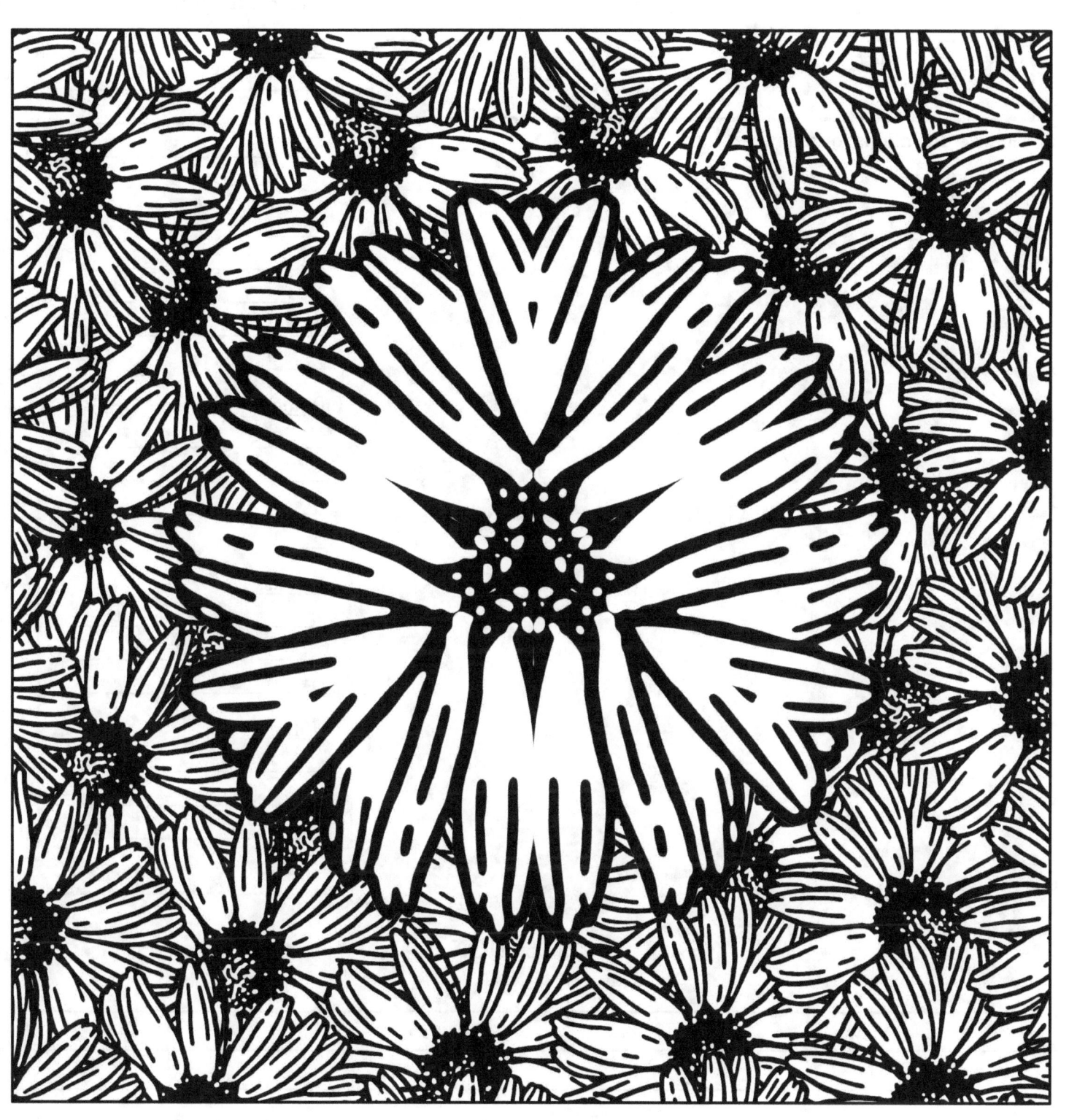

Morning thoughts:

_____
_____
_____
_____
_____
_____
_____

DATE: _____

Food

Water: IIII IIII IIII

<u>Breakfast:</u>
_____
_____
_____
_____

<u>Lunch:</u>
_____
_____
_____
_____

<u>Dinner:</u>
_____
_____
_____
_____

<u>Snacks:</u>
_____
_____

<u>Notes:</u>
_____
_____
_____

Goals & Intentions for today

1

2

3

4

5

6

GRATITUDE

REFLECTION

_____
_____
_____
_____
_____

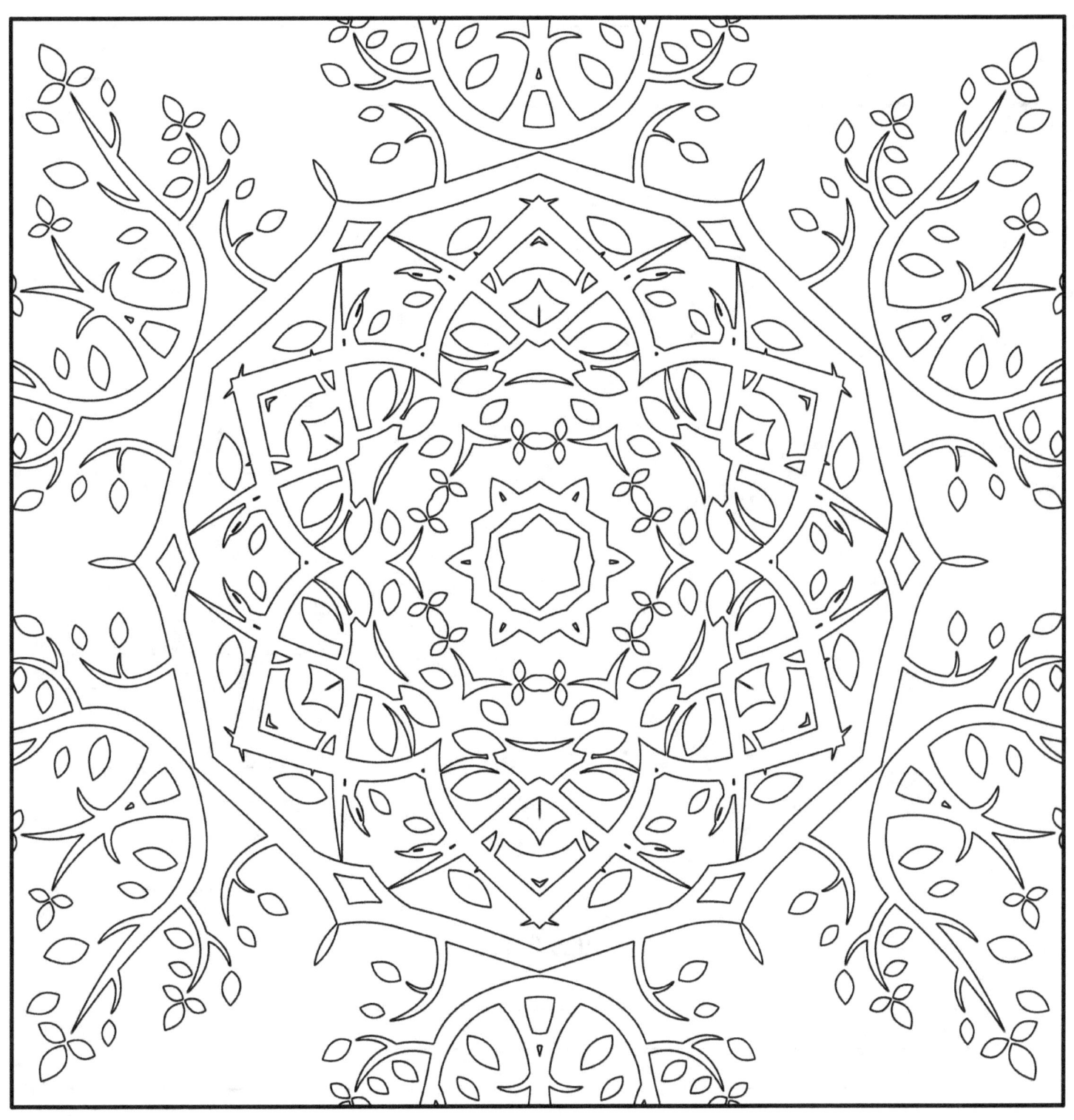

Morning thoughts:

_____
_____
_____
_____
_____
_____
_____

DATE:
_____

Food

Water: IIII IIII IIII

<u>Breakfast:</u>
_____
_____
_____
_____

<u>Lunch:</u>
_____
_____
_____
_____

<u>Dinner:</u>
_____
_____
_____
_____

<u>Snacks:</u>
_____
_____
_____

<u>Notes:</u>
_____
_____
_____

Goals & Intentions for today

1
2
3
4
5
6

GRATITUDE

REFLECTION

_____
_____
_____
_____
_____

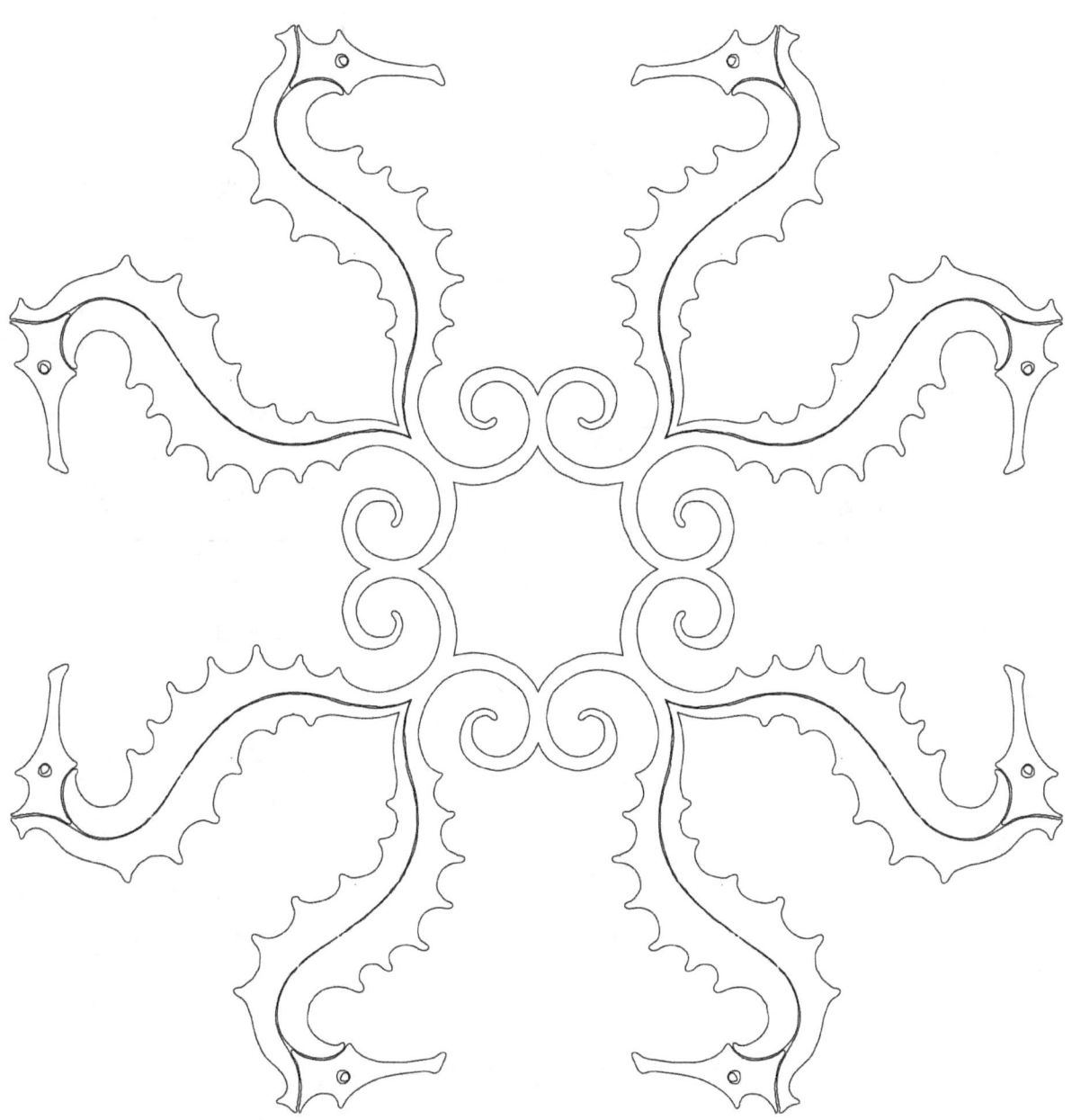

Morning thoughts:
_____
_____
_____
_____
_____
_____
_____

DATE:
_____

Food

Water: IIII IIII IIII

<u>Breakfast:</u>
_____
_____
_____
____

<u>Lunch:</u>
_____
_____
_____
____

<u>Dinner:</u>
_____
_____
_____
____

<u>Snacks:</u>
_____
_____
_____

<u>Notes:</u>
_____
_____
_____
_____

Goals & Intentions for today

1
2
3
4
5
6

GRATITUDE

REFLECTION

_____
_____
_____
_____
_____

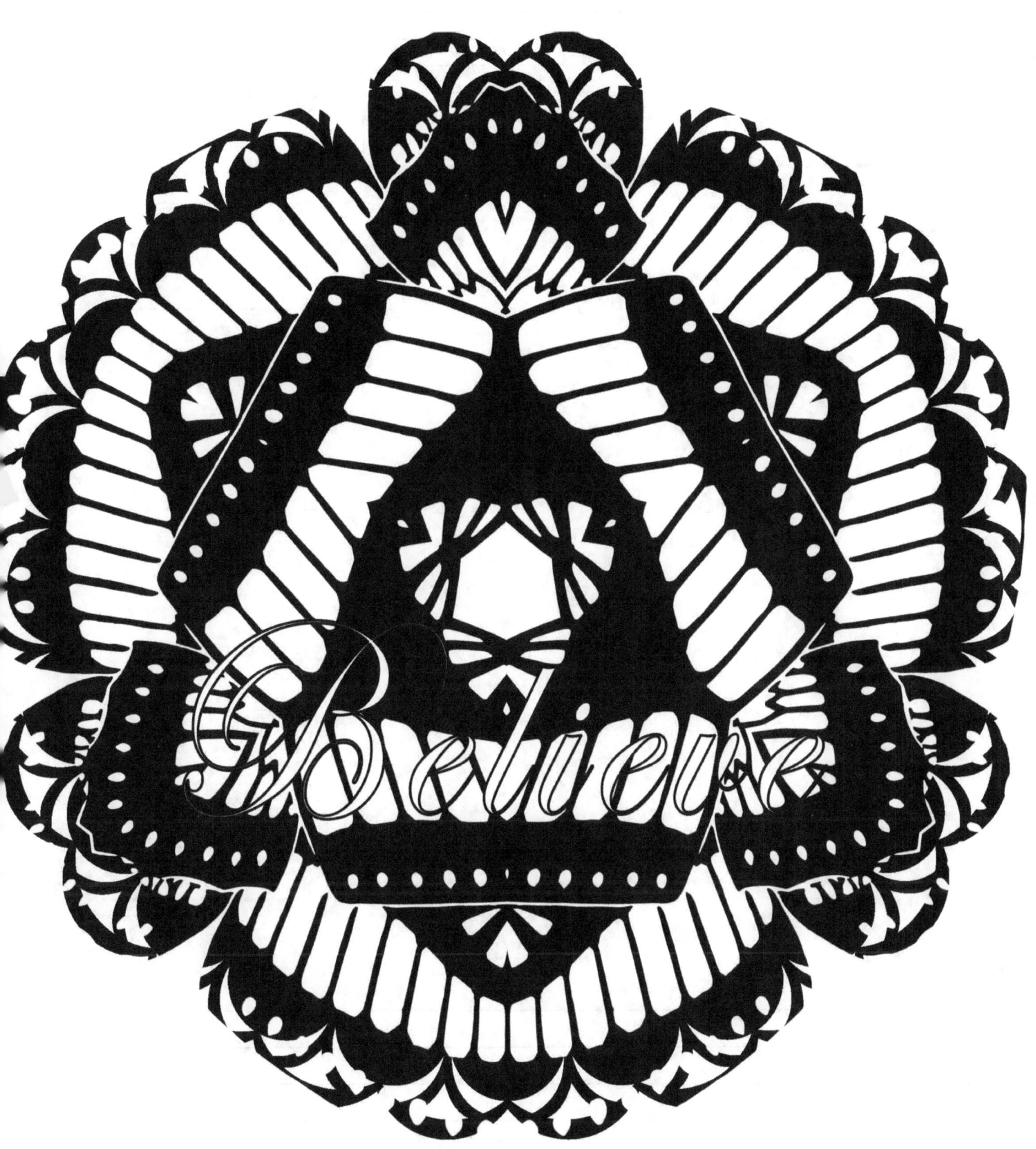

Morning thoughts:

_____
_____
_____
_____
_____
_____
_____

DATE:
_____

Goals & Intentions for today

1

2

3

4

5

6

GRATITUDE

Food

Water: IIII IIII IIII

Breakfast:
_____
_____
_____
_____

Lunch:
_____
_____
_____

Dinner:
_____
_____
_____

Snacks:
_____
_____

Notes:
_____
_____

REFLECTION

_____
_____
_____
_____
_____

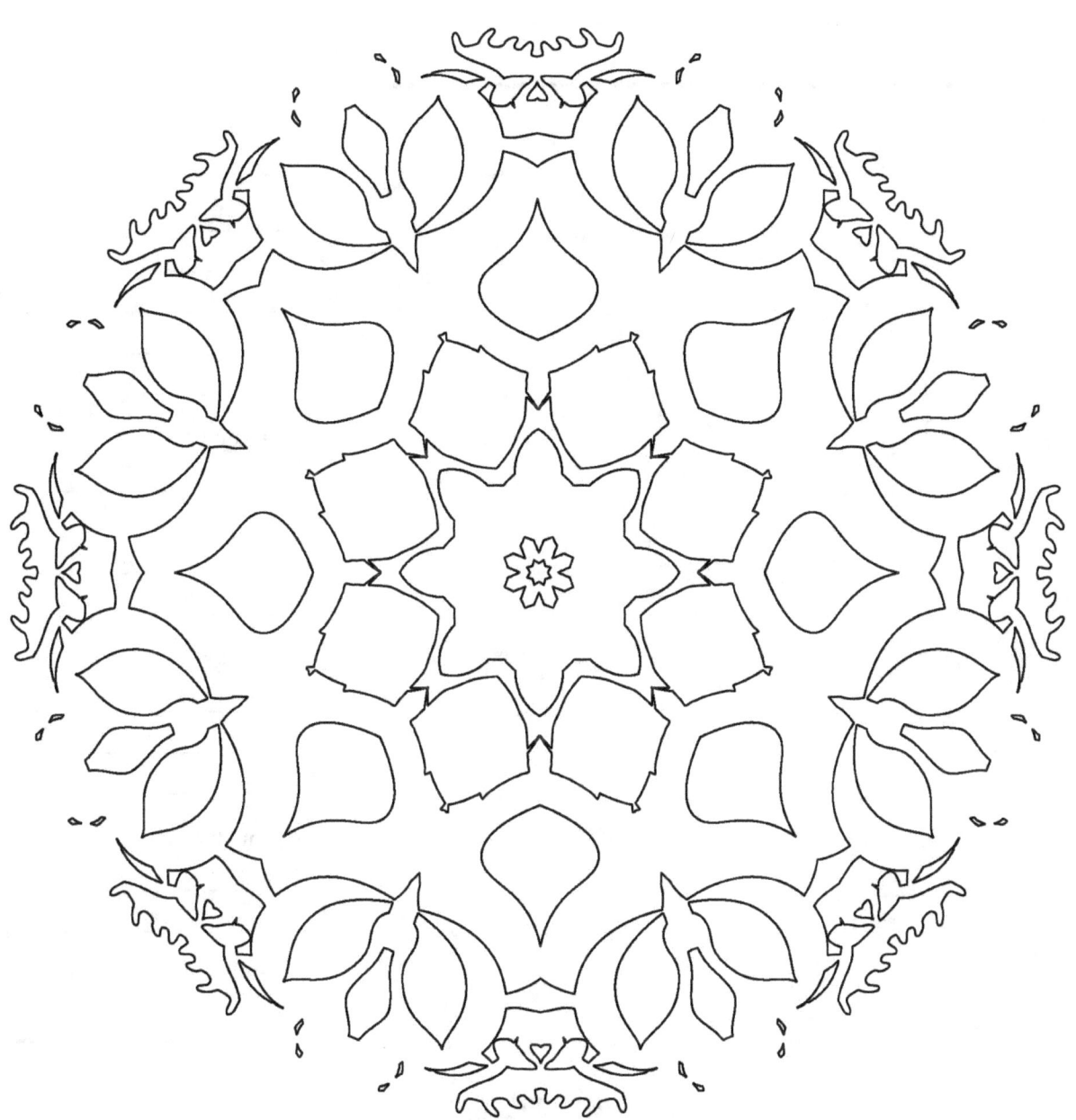

Morning thoughts:

_____
_____
_____
_____
_____
_____
_____

DATE:
_____

Food

Water: IIII IIII IIII

<u>Breakfast:</u>
_____
_____
_____
_____

Goals & Intentions for today

1

2

3

4

5

6

<u>Lunch:</u>
_____
_____
_____
_____

<u>Dinner:</u>
_____
_____
_____
_____

GRATITUDE

<u>Snacks:</u>
_____
_____
_____

<u>Notes:</u>
_____
_____
_____
_____

REFLECTION

_____
_____
_____
_____
_____

MomPositive Health Coaching Resources

To contact Tammi please email or use a contact form from one of her websites below.

Want more? Tammi wants to share more with you! Be sure you stop by her website to down load free guides, get free recipes, schedule a free fifty minute consultation, and learn more about living MomPositively!

www.headpositivemom.com

I am here to help you succeed!

Tammi Hoerner, INHC

tammihoerner@gmail.com
www.headpositivemom.com

Follow Tammi on Facebook at: https://www.facebook.com/tammi.hoerner

Follow Tammi on Pinterest at: https://www.pinterest.com/tammihoerner/

Additional Resources:

The Institute for Integrative Nutrition

Learn more about being an Integrative Nutrition Health Coach here: http://geti.in/1wfnjHA